I CROSSED THE MINCH

Louis MacNeice was born in Belfast in 1907 and educated at Sherborne, Marlborough, and Merton College, Oxford. Poet, playwright, BBC producer and feature writer, translator, critic and university lecturer, MacNeice's literary reputation was for too long overshadowed by that of his friend W. H. Auden. But since his death in 1963 at the age of fifty-five, MacNeice's stature has steadily grown. Thanks mainly to the advocacy of poets from the North of Ireland (in particular Paul Muldoon, Seamus Heaney and Michael Longley) MacNeice is now regarded as the key figure who, along with Patrick Kavanagh, provides a bridge between W. B. Yeats and contemporary Irish poets. There is little doubt that he is, as fellow Belfast-born poet Derek Mahon has described him, 'one of the giants of modern poetry'.

Tom Herron is Lecturer in English in the School of Cultural Studies at Leeds Metropolitan University.

The Author

I CROSSED THE MINCH

LOUIS MACNEICE

With eight drawings by
NANCY SHARP

Polygon

First published in 1938 by Longmans, Green and Co.
This edition published in Great Britain in 2007 by
Polygon, an imprint of Birlinn Ltd
West Newington House
10 Newington Road
Edinburgh
EH9 1QS
www.birlinn.co.uk

ISBN 10: 1 84697 014 8
ISBN 13: 978 1 84697 014 6

Illustrations by Nancy Sharp courtesy of the
Trustees of the National Library of Scotland

British Library Cataloguing-in-Publication Data
A catalogue record for this book is available
on request from the British Library.

Typeset in Great Britain by Antony Gray
Printed and bound by Creative Print and Design,
Ebbw Vale, Wales

CONTENTS

LIST OF ILLUSTRATIONS

INTRODUCTION

> I AM very sorry that I know no Gaelic. Before visiting the Hebrides I did not realise that nearly all the islanders speak Gaelic and that their language is integral to their life. Owing to my ignorance of their language I was unable to become intimate with the lives of the people. This book consequently is a tripper's book written by someone who was disappointed and tantalised by the islands and seduced by them only to be reminded that on that soil he will always be an outsider. I doubt if I shall visit the Western Islands again.

So begins Louis MacNeice's account of the two journeys he made, in the spring and summer of 1937, through the Western Isles of Scotland. MacNeice was, by his own admission, spectacularly ill-suited for such an assignment but, needing the money and flattered 'that publishers should ask me to do something unsuitable', he took the train from London to the North West of Scotland, and then crossed the Minch – the strait of water separating the mainland from the Outer Hebrides – and proceeded to travel by bus, car, plane, boat, and on foot through the archipelago of islands.

Following loosely in the footsteps of Johnson and

Boswell, and armed with a quarter-inch map of Skye and the Outer Islands, and a MacBrayne's ferry timetable MacNeice travelled through the Western Isles in an unflagging performance of a tourist passing too quickly through places and lives he knew little about.

It would be erroneous to suggest that MacNeice's reading matter on his two trips to the Western Isles indicated a total immersion in Scottish or Hebridean culture: he took with him 'a very un-Hebridean book', *The Notebooks and Papers of Gerard Manley Hopkins*' (1937), Federico García Lorca's *Lament for a Bullfighter* (1935), and Cecil Day-Lewis's *The Mind in Chains* (1937). In addition, it is inconceivable that he did not take along with him a copy of Johnson and Boswell's *Journey to the Western Islands of Scotland* (originally published in 1775).

Asked by the friend of a friend, 'How can you expect to write this book if you are not steeped in the history of the place?' MacNeice replied, 'I have a slight conscience about that myself, but my public, such as it is, won't care if I know the history or not.' MacNeice's honesty on the matter is disarming and at the same time slightly unnerving: a reader opening the newly published *I Crossed the Minch* may well have wondered to herself, 'What, exactly, *is* this book?' It is certainly not a travel guide in the conventional sense: indeed, MacNeice advises his reader not to follow him out to the Hebrides:

> the tourist is himself a corruption. If you must visit the islands, visit Skye, the largest island of Scotland which is already recognised as a playground for English hikers and mountaineers. The population of Skye is dwindling

> steadily but that will not worry the mountaineers who prefer to mountaineer in desolation. And anglers I should advise to leave the Outer Islands alone. The people in North and South Uist do not like your presence. You will not know what they are saying but they will damn you to hell in Gaelic . . . The natives will not welcome you enthusiastically. They will be polite, considerate and hospitable, but they will be able to get along better without you than with you; they have not yet acquired the Blackpool mentality.

And if, on opening *I Crossed the Minch*, the reader was expecting vivid and enticing descriptions of the wild landsapes and the charmingly quaint people of the Hebrides she would be equally disappointed:

> Most books about the Highlands and Islands steep the landscape in uncontrollable purples and golds and sentimentalise the people. From what I have seen . . . the landscape of the Outer Hebrides is not unusually rich or varied in colour and the people lack that more blatant surface-charm or glamour – that sugared folkiness – which we are led to expect in out-of-the-way places by travelogues and Geographical magazines. Nor are the Hebrideans good-looking.

Stylistically too, *I Crossed the Minch* is difficult to pin down. It is a glorious hybrid of elements: travel narrative; journal entries; exchanges between imaginary characters; passages of local history; personal auto-biography and childhood reminiscences; witty letters to friends (W. H. Auden in particular); anecdotes; literary parodies; complaints about the food, the weather, the local dogs, and much else; slightly forced invectives against landlords and landlordism; rather primitive sketches done by his travelling partner, Nancy Sharp (who is never once mentioned in the book); and, of course, poems, including 'Bagpipe Music', 'Leaving Barra' and 'On those Islands'. Indeed, it is this promiscuous hybridity that may account for the book's relatively obscure status in comparison, say, to *Letters from Iceland* (1937), the travel book MacNeice co-wrote with Auden. Whereas *Letters from Iceland* has remained in print, *I Crossed the Minch* ran to only two editions. After its 1939 reissue in a cloth-bound edition it fell into obscurity, known only to MacNeice scholars, and virtually unavailable, until now, to a wider audience. The location of the manuscript is unknown: it does not feature in any of the major MacNeice archives. Jon Stallworthy believes it may well have been destroyed by MacNeice himself. A further possibility is that it perished when the offices of Longmans, Green & Co. on Paternoster Row were destroyed by German bombs in 1940.

So why did MacNeice's Hebridean travel book sink more or less without trace so soon after its composition? There are several possible reasons: one may be that *I Crossed the Minch* is simply not as good a book as *Letters from Iceland*. While I'd dispute this in terms of the whole book, there are, admittedly, certain weak moments in it: the conversations with Crowder and Perceval, MacNeice's imaginary metropolitan chums, stand out as particularly irritating, if not altogether uninteresting.

Another reason could be that Auden (always, of course, the greater figure in terms of literary reputations) guaranteed a greater potential readership than a book produced solely by the relatively unknown MacNeice who, before *Letters from Iceland*, had published only two volumes of poetry, one play and one translation. A further reason could be the fact that yet another book of observations and anecdotes by an outsider travelling through the Scottish Highlands and Islands was hardly likely to make a lasting impression – all the more so as the 1930s and 1940s saw a veritable explosion of such writing. Published almost exclusively by London publishing houses, this writing was intimately connected to the development during those decades of tourism in the more 'remote' parts of Britain and Ireland. While *I Crossed the Minch* has something in common with Owen Hamilton's *Hebridean Holiday* (1936), Alasdair Alpin MacGregor's *Hebridean Journey* (1939), F. Fraser Darling's *Island Years* (1940), Margaret Leigh's *Driftwood and Tangle* (1941), Seton Gordon's *Highways and Byways in the West Highlands* (1935), Iain F. Anderson's *To Introduce the Hebrides* (1933) and *Across Hebridean Seas* (1937), Norman Nicholson's *Hebridean Lore and Romance* (1937) and John Lorne Campbell's *The Book of Barra* (1936), it is a more complex and hard-edged book than any of them. In fact it is closer in spirit (and style) to later, markedly more critical portraits of the islands such as Alasdair Alpin MacGregor's notorious *The Western Islands* (1949) and Hugh MacDiarmid's *The Islands of Scotland: Hebrides, Orkneys, and Shetlands* (1939). Like MacNeice, MacDiarmid wrote *The Islands of Scotland* mainly as a means of making some money. But his uncompromising portrait of the islands was not well received and the book quickly went out of print. And like *I Crossed the Minch*, MacDiarmid's book is an interweaving of travel description with poetry. It is interesting to note the extent to which both MacDiarmid and MacGregor were themselves clearly indebted to a book of observations and opinions on their fellow countrymen and country-women produced by a Marlborough- and Merton-educated Anglo-Irish Protestant from Belfast.

While I think there is much to commend each or even all of these reasons for the low, or barely existent, profile of *I Crossed the Minch*, I prefer to take a somewhat different, and altogether more sympathetic view. *I Crossed the Minch* is an uncategorisable book. Neither a travel guide (MacNeice detested the genre) nor an anthropological or physical description of the islands, it is essentially a record of an outsider's search for connections and origins in the Celtic Fringe, and as such it scarcely fulfils the brief MacNeice received from Longmans to write a book about the Western Isles, just as it most probably frustrates every expectation of a reader expecting to open a book of descriptions of the islands' landscapes and people. *I Crossed the Minch* is much more interesting than that. It is a quest narrative in a minor key, all the more fascinating because the failure of the quest is executed in a magnificent stylistic, thematic and tonal promiscuity.

A kind of touristic nomad or expropriated flâneur, MacNeice is guided on his journeys by a mixture of whim, the all-pervading textual influence of Dr Johnson, and advice from his friend Hector MacIver, to whom the book itself, and the very fine poem 'Leaving Barra', are dedicated. Writer, broadcaster and friend of MacNeice, MacIver is a constant presence in *I Crossed the Minch*. Not only did he set out, over haggis and whisky in Edinburgh, MacNeice's travel itinerary, he shaped many of the writer's attitudes whilst on the islands: 'debunk the landlords . . . uncultured tyrants!' MacIver urges MacNeice, who promises that he will do just that if he meets any.

While no expert on the Hebrides, MacNeice is by no means entirely ignorant of the circumstances affecting the lives of the people he meets on Lewis, Harris, North Uist, Barra, Coll and Tiree. Unlike most of the detested English tourists he comes across in the better hotels in the islands, MacNeice goes out of his way – normally on foot – to talk to people: schoolteachers, travelling salesmen, crofters, writers, singers and fellow drinkers in the bars and hotels he frequents provide a flow of information about the islands. The fallout from Lord Leverhulme's grandiose plans for the islands, the impact of chronic under-employment and emigration, the shift in the tweed industry from croft-based production to large-scale mechanised production, the baneful effects of absentee landlordism, the threat to the local fishing industry from foreign fishing fleets, the questionable benefits of tourism, the spectre of another pan-European war – all of these are registered, albeit fleetingly, by MacNeice.

To be fair, these issues were not really of primary concern to him: they were not the reasons for his visit to the islands. Apart from the need to make some money (he made £75 from the book), he had other less tangible but very definite reasons for visiting the Western Isles; one was his life-long need to attach himself to a certain idea of place, culture and people. Few poets have worked as hard as MacNeice to establish a myth of origin:

> from a very early age I began to long for something different, to construct various dreams . . . The first of these dream worlds was 'The West of Ireland', a phrase which still stirs me, if not like a trumpet, like a fiddle half heard through a cattle fair. My parents came from that West or, more precisely, from Connemara, and it was obvious that both of them vastly preferred it to Ulster. The very name Connemara seemed too rich for any ordinary place. It appeared to be a country of windswept open spaces and mountains blazing with whins and seas that were never quiet, with drowned palaces beneath them, and seals and eagles and turf smoke and cottagers who were always laughing and who gave you milk when you asked for a glass of water. And the people's voices were different there, soft and rich like my father's . . . But I was not to visit Achill or Connemara until I had left school. So for many years I lived on a nostalgia for somewhere I had never been. ('Landscapes of Childhood and Youth: (Pages from an Unwritten Book)', *The Strings are False*, London: Faber, 1965)

MacNeice is undisguised in his desire to forge connections: 'I went to the Hebrides partly hoping to find that blood was thicker than ink – that the Celt in me would be drawn to the surface by the magnetism of his fellows. This was a sentimental and futile hope.'

It was indeed. MacNeice's miscalculation colours everything he sees and does in the Western Isles. Expecting to find them 'like the West of Ireland – a wild landscape and a genial people', the Hebrides are disappointing to him precisely because they are not that West of Ireland, because they are not part of that idealised backwater so beloved of celticists and romantic nationalists. One suspects that MacNeice might have been slightly happier had he found the Hebrides in a state somewhat closer to that of the Aran Islands when John Millington Synge made his pilgrimages there in the final years of the nineteenth century (see *The Aran Islands*, Dublin: Maunsell & Co; London: Elkin Mathews, 1907). What makes *I Crossed the Minch* so fascinating is the way in which the author reveals, in the very act of attempting to establish connections with the landscape and the people of the Western Isles, the absurd and entirely mythical nature of such longings. There's a lesson here for all travel writers, and even all travellers, who look to certain places as unsullied or 'authentic' eutopias immune to, in W. B. Yeats's phrase, 'the filthy modern tide' of commerce, industrialisation and modernisation. MacNeice went in search of a eutopia conjured mainly out of his own imaginative attachment to all things celtic and western, but found a society beset by emigration and economic decline while at the same time struggling to survive as a viable cultural entity. In much the same way as Synge found Aran to be succumbing to mainstream capitalist society, the Hebrides, too, turned out to be inadequately exotic for MacNeice. *I Crossed the Minch* –

for its exuberant hybridity, its outrageous judgements, its urbane wit and its genuine insights – is a record of that disappointment.

MacNeice's disillusionment is not, however, the whole story of *I Crossed the Minch*: it is not the fate of the Western Isles to be his *tristes tropiques* (Declan Kiberd's memorable description – *pace* Claude Lévi-Strauss – of Synge's overwhelmingly melancholic disposition towards the Aran Islands). Once he realises that he is in a culture that is not meekly acquiescent to his personal mythopoesis, and in a place that is not merely a faded facsimile of the West of Ireland, he allows himself to be a tourist with all the freedoms and limitations that the role implies. And like any tourist, MacNeice looks at things quickly and partially and, often, with barely any reflection. The famous standing stones at Callanish, for example, are visited but they provoke only the most lukewarm of responses: 'They were very much what I expected. But they seemed all right of their kind.' MacNeice's chief pleasures are in his mammoth walks (the first in April, across the hills from Loch Morsgail in Lewis to Tarbert in Harris, and the second in July, when he walks joyously and, at times, deliriously through heavy rain all the way from Loch Seaforth to Loch Erisort in Lewis) and in those moments when companionship and alcohol achieve a near-perfect balance. The most memorable incident occurs at the annual sports day at Barvas: MacNeice describes with directness and vividness a few hours in the summer of 1937 and invests them with something approaching the actual, laced with just a trace of the mythical:

> Children sat on the crisp turf sucking ice cornets . . . The air was very mild . . . All the young men in cloth caps offered each other Capstan cigarettes. A Celtic timelessness suffused the scene like sunshine . . . I smoked several cigarettes and bought some liquorice sweets. The people all around me were happy and voluble in Gaelic. After an hour or two a car arrived with some pipers. The pipers mixed with the crowd and talked to their friends, but revealed no intention of piping. Young men in football jerseys loitered around looking for an event. No events took place. The sun went on shining on the moors and the brown River Barvas.

Moments such as this provide one of the chief pleasures of reading *I Crossed the Minch* seventy years removed from the world described by MacNeice. This and other passages – a walk through Shawbost accompanied by the euphony of numerous looms producing tweed, or sleeping in the sun at Arnabost in Coll as peewits circle overhead, or setting out from Stornoway on an over-night fishing trip on a drifter – constitute a small-scale social history of a world that has now receded into history. To be sure, MacNeice is no cultural historian, but his vividness of observation, his eagerness to talk to the many people he meets, his openness to what the Hebrides have to offer, and his clear-eyed knowledge of his outsider status, combine to produce a book that more than holds it own in the canon of travel-writing devoted to the Highlands and Islands of Scotland.

Tom Herron
Edinburgh, June 2007

I CROSSED
THE MINCH

TO

HECTOR MACIVER

DEAR HECTOR,

I do not suppose you will like this—the book of an outsider who has treated frivolously what he could not assess on its merits. May I thank you for the kindness of the Islands.

Yours ever,

LOUIS MACNEICE.

PART I

VISIT IN APRIL

I

INTRODUCTORY

I AM very sorry that I know no Gaelic. Before visiting the Hebrides I did not realise that nearly all the islanders speak Gaelic and that their language is integral to their life. Owing to my ignorance of their language I was unable to become intimate with the lives of the people. This book consequently is a tripper's book written by someone who was disappointed and tantalised by the islands and seduced by them only to be reminded that on that soil he will always be an outsider. I doubt if I shall visit the Western Islands again.

Apart from my sentimental reluctance to be an outsider I do not wish to visit them again because they are in a decline. London also is in a decline, but there I feel that I am present at a family sickbed—if not indeed a family deathbed. By blood I may be nearer to a Hebridean than to a cockney, but my whole upbringing has alienated me from that natural (some will call it primitive) culture which in the British Isles today is only found on the Celtic or backward fringes. I went to the Hebrides partly hoping to find that blood was thicker than ink—that the Celt in me would be drawn to the surface by the magnetism of his fellows. This was a sentimental and futile hope. Once, sitting by a river drinking beer with some Lewismen while one of them sang a love-song in Gaelic, I felt strongly that I belonged to these people and that, for all I cared, London could sink in the mud. But the conviction of alcohol does not last. The next day in Stornoway I rushed to the stationer's to try to buy a copy of the *Listener*.

QUESTION: What did you listen to?

ANSWER: I listened to the voice of London enunciating facts for the masses with a soi-disant impartiality. I heard my late landlord in Birmingham, a professor of economics, discuss the industrial Midlands. I heard an art critic whom I know discuss the portrait of a writer whom I know, painted by a painter whom I know. And the glorious fact dawned on me that really I knew everybody. I knew hardly a soul in the Hebrides, but that's not where *everybody* lives. How lovely to belong to that wider civilisation—how lovely to belong to that clique!

An island means isolation; the words are the same. We expect in an island to meet with insular vices. What is shocking is to find an island invaded by the vices of the mainland. The Hebrides are now being invaded by commerce, which means that they are falling to the foreigner. This process may be inevitable but I should prefer to watch it somewhere where it is further advanced, where differences of wealth are of long standing and where, though the primitive culture has gone, a sophisticated culture has succeeded it. More than one generation is required before a man can be a capitalist with grace.

I heard of a small crofter in one of the islands who cornered the local tweed industry. This was not a nice Arnold Bennett romance of the poor boy making good. The Poor Boy made twenty thousand but he and his family seem merely to have improved themselves financially while the community which gave rise to them is, thanks to their triumph, losing independence and character. A hundred and sixty looms in two small villages work for this man alone. The hundred and sixty families who used to make their tweed independently, are now bound by contract to a tyrant; the manner of their work, the amount of their output, are imposed upon them from outside. They all use mechanical steel looms which turn out at least twice the amount of cloth in the time but not such a good cloth as the wooden hand-loom. The wool comes to them from the factories ready dyed and all that they have to do is the weaving. The crofters no longer spin or dye the wool and, when it is woven, they no longer waulk the tweed. The decay of these arts means the disappearance of the songs which attended them—the spinning songs and waulking songs. It means, more widely, a great lessening of the worker's pride in his work. Quantity has ousted quality.

The tradition in the islands is that a man lives on his land but by what he gets out of the sea. In the eyes of the world, however, the fisherman-crofter is superannuated. And the world sends up its trawlers to sweep the fish out of the Minch. The islanders of Lewis defeated Lord Leverhulme who wanted them to sacrifice the traditions for an organised commercial prosperity. But it is easier to defeat someone who attends to you than someone who ignores you. The world is going to kill the last of the Celts by ignoring them.

Yet I will not suggest that you save the islands by visiting them. For the tourist is himself a corruption. If you must visit the islands, visit Skye, the largest island of Scotland which is already recognised as a playground for English hikers and mountaineers. The population of Skye is dwindling steadily but that will not worry the mountaineers who prefer to mountaineer in desolation. And anglers I should advise to leave the Outer Islands alone. The people in North and South Uist do not like your presence. You will not know what they are saying but they will damn you to hell in Gaelic. A Gaelic-speaking friend of mine, when having a drink at Pollachar in South Uist, was mistaken for an English angler and heard himself damned into pieces:

When I first visited the islands, I was impertinent enough to resent what I considered the dourness of many of the inhabitants. Most English visitors are sure to be equally impertinent. The natives will not welcome you enthusiastically. They will be polite, considerate and hospitable, but they will be able to get along better without you than with you; they have not yet acquired the Blackpool mentality. The seventh Duke of Argyll in a pamphlet (1883) defending his management of his estate in the island of Tiree looked forward to the day when the place would be a paradise for visitors and properly equipped with golf courses.

QUESTION: Where will the natives be then, poor things?

ANSWER: Oh, they will be the caddies.

The Hebrideans are slow of movement like most

peasants and fishermen. But they are not slow of speech or mind as the visitor thinks who can only speak to them in English. Most of them pick their way uncomfortably through English, slowly and heavily, without much expression. But listen to them speaking Gaelic and you will notice that they speak with fire, speed and dramatic variety. In the same way when dealing with a foreigner they appear very undemonstrative but I have seen them greet their own near neighbours with a warmth of hand-clasping and kissing which we reserve for our relations back from the tropics. In many of them their religion, especially the Free Church brand, has cramped their vitality. But a friend of mine who comes from Lewis tells me that in the typical Lewisman Presbyterianism and 'Scottish' respectability are only skin-deep. Apply whiskey and you will notice the resurgence of the Catholic and the Celt.

And Presbyterian morality is not always as harsh as it is painted. There are many illegitimate children in the islands. Their mothers are by most people not looked down on but merely considered silly. The child is usually given the surname of its father though it is a rare thing for the father to marry the mother. A woman living in one of the islands has seven illegitimate children with six surnames between them. In the same way by no means all the islanders are extremist about the sabbath. A friend of mine who worked as a labourer in Mull, used to spend his Sundays writing. This was condoned but when he introduced a typewriter, the woman of the house expostulated—'Aren't ye afraid to use that machine? Don't ye think the Lord will hear ye?'

Most books about the Highlands and Islands steep the landscape in uncontrolled purples and golds and sentimentalise the people. From what I have seen on two visits, one in April and one in July, the landscape of the Outer Islands is not unusually rich or varied in colour and the people lack that more blatant surface-charm or glamour—that sugared folkiness—which we are led to expect in out-of-the-way places by travelogues and Geographical Magazines. Nor are the Hebrideans good-looking. Their facial expression is more pleasing than that of the Lowland Scot but, like most Scots, their features are raw and imperfect. Some of the older women have a massive facial dignity due to prominent cheekbones and years of manual work. A few have a Madonna-like beauty but the Madonna quality is usually lost by a disproportionate length of chin and by the fact that they have ceased wearing the head-shawl. The landscape also would be more striking if there were more whins, as there are in Ireland, but whins are discouraged as the sheep tend to get caught in them. Wild flowers are plentiful in July. Not being a flower-lover proper I preferred the larger effects—emerald strips of oats coiling on the hills like snakes or a three-acre meadow purple with wild geraniums.

Most visitors to the Hebrides comment pityingly on the inertia of the inhabitants who refuse to develop their land scientifically or to apply modern methods of agriculture. But science presupposes a special and modern methods presuppose a great deal of money. Or do you expect that a crofter who finds it difficult to pay a rent of two pounds a year will be able to get a steam tractor on credit and pay for it out of his profits? And in many parts of the Hebrides it is doubtful whether modern methods would be applicable. No machine could tackle the rugged slopes which are turned by hand into 'lazy-beds'. A benefactor has lately established a model farm near Stornoway in Lewis where peat-land is by an elaborate process rendered arable. But it seems unlikely that this process would be feasible on a large scale. And the islanders would be adverse to any reform which might, directly or indirectly, endanger their rights to the land.

I could not bear, in the fishing-hotels, hearing people patronise the improvident natives whose lakes and rivers they were plundering. Yet it must be admitted that the islanders, like the Southern Irish, show a disregard for time and for penny-in-the-slot efficiency. When I visited the annual sports at Barvas in Lewis an hour seemed regularly to elapse between one event and the next. And at some places the cows are not milked before ten in the morning. There is a charming little poem directed at this trait of the Highlanders:

> O that the peats might cut themselves
>   And the fish chump on the shore,
> That I might lie upon my bed
>   And sleep for evermore!

It is perhaps fairer to take these lines as the expression of that dream of a Schlaraffenland which is proper to all who work upon the land.

Many people in the Outer Islands are Scottish Nationalists. I have always laughed at Scottish Nationalism as a precious affectation of bright young men with a distaste for real politics, but in the islands the concepthas more meaning than it has in Edinburgh. Scotland as a whole will never regain a vital self-consciousness of her unity and individuality, but such a thing is still just possible for the Gaelic-speaking islands as a group in separation from the mainland. Their traditional language needs no artificial cultivation, their population is small enough to allow of a genuine community feeling, their social life is still homogeneous (though commercialisation may soon drive rifts through it), lastly the sea still separates them from their neighbours:

ἔστιν θάλασσα, τίς δὲ νιν κατασβέσει;

Nationalism of the Irish type is often regarded as reactionary. With the World Revolution and the Classless Society waiting for the midwife, why take a torch to the stable to assist at the birth of a puppy? Even if the puppy is pedigree. On this question I am unable to make up my mind. When I am in Ireland I find myself becoming Nationalist. If I lived in the Hebrides, I should certainly plump for the puppy.

Are the family, the local community, the clique community of ideas, personal relationships, even persons themselves, to be jettisoned in order that Collective Man may keep floating? I think not. They may change their outward appearance, may throw away their military boots, their heavy luggage, the irrevelant accumulation of centuries, but if they throw themselves into the sea, if they all insist on playing Jonah, who is to be left in the boat? I look out over the waves and see a trim craft riding them lightly—rather too lightly to be true. And as it comes nearer, I see that it is entirely empty—polished decks, everything trim and shipshape, no offence to ideology, but where the hell are the people? Oh they have all committed *hara-kiri*, were conscious of original sin; the poor dears were too individual.

So many left-wing comrades, at least in England, suffer from the masochism of the puritan. No frills, they say, no comforts, no luxuries of body or mind. No differences between person and person or community and community which could possibly impede the understanding of one by the other, the co-operation of one with the other in forwarding the march of history and singing the one creed in unison. A future of Esperanto, Sunday School treats and homage to the Highest Common Factor. Not that this was Lenin's ideal, who saw clearly that differentiation is necessary; only it must not be founded on the irrelevant accident of birth or the luck of money.

It is an admirable hope that the peoples of the world shall understand one another and that one man shall understand his neighbour but not if there is nothing to understand. Any development means differentiation. It is only by keeping people's minds at a low stage of development—a low standard of thinking—that you can achieve a society where poetry, say, or music or mathematics can be fairly distributed to all. A hen's egg, if it had cognition, would feel more at home among duck's eggs than a hen would feel at home among ducks. But you can't put the clock back once the chickens are fledged. You can't say to the hens and ducks, 'You rotters! What do you mean by establishing these artificial differences—web-feet and wattles—what do you mean by sacrificing that original pattern which once was visible in both of you—that bald and oval purity of design?'

A world society must be a federation of differentiated communities, not a long line of robots doing the goose-step. In the same way the community itself must be a community of individuals. Only they must not be fake individuals—archaizers and dilettantes—any more than the community must be a fake community, a totalitarian state strutting in the museum robes of Caesardom. The Soviet Union, I am told, encourages the maintenance of local traditions and culture though in subservience to the new order. Such is the proper programme for historical development. If you are in the middle of a bridge, it is silly to blow up the part behind you before you have crossed. And if there are several bridges across a river, you may as well use the one which is nearest to hand.

It would be absurd to suggest that the Hebrides should attempt to be self-supporting—economically independent. (No one, as far as I know, has yet introduced into the Hebrides the bogey of beet-sugar with its accompanying chorus of rats.) Some compromise, however, should be possible which would preserve the islands' social and cultural independence. Economically they should be allowed to adjust themselves to their bigger neighbours without kowtowing to them. I do not for a moment suggest that, in order to retain their language and community feeling, they should deliberately refuse the advantages of modernisation. I met some Lewismen who deplored the recent establishment of bus services. Obviously when a Lewisman can get from Uig to Ness any day of the week in two or three hours by bus, the old differences between the Ness man and the Uig man will become much less marked and a certain amount that is locally of value will be lost. The differences between the Uig man and the Ness man are much less important than what they have in common or than what the inhabitants of the whole group of islands have in common and in contrast to most Scotsmen on the mainland. Some day it may be a good thing that the Hebrideans should lose their language and be in every way amalgamated with the rest of Scotland or (as the case may be) with all the English-speaking races of the world. But that day is not yet. The ill-effects of rapid anglicisation can be seen in the town of Stornoway. The crofter comes to town to swap his traditional rhythm and routine for the fussy mentality of Glasgow and the jerky culture of an English public library.

For two centuries the natives of the Hebrides have been encouraged to emigrate, often by the false promises of hypocrite landlords. Dr. Johnson in 1773 deplored the wholesale emigration which was then going on from the islands—'It may be thought that they are happier by the change; but they are not happy as a nation, for they are a nation no longer. As they contribute not to the prosperity of any community, they must want that security, that dignity, that happiness, whatever it be, which a prosperous community throws back upon individuals.'

The Hebrides now do not suffer from poverty. As a crofter in Lewis said to me, 'You can't really say in a crofting community that people are *hard up*.' And if one man in a village finds it hard to get enough to eat, his neighbours will help him out. At the same time unemployment and unsatisfactory conditions of labour are impoverishing the people spiritually. And neither the over-population of Lewis nor the under-population of Skye presents a rural Utopia.

You will find in this book no picture of island Utopias. I have gone sparingly with the gilt and the whitewash. I hope that some native of the Hebrides will soon write a book about them which will do justice to their noble traditions and be at the same time an effective polemic against disintegrating influences. I am not qualified to write either such a polemic or such a eulogy. This is the book of a tripper, a person concerned with the surface. In my study of the surface I have had the invaluable assistance of two young men whom I would not describe as my friends but with whom I have much in common.

These two persons (who are *not* taken from the life and for this I tender them apologies) first turned up when my train for Edinburgh was a little way out from Euston. I was looking out of the window at the dreary rows of houses with the chimneys held up like the hands of a man surrendering, when I sensed the two alien presences. They had taken the two corner seats opposite. Crowder as usual was wearing plus fours and in a somewhat smug good humour after a couple of pints of bitter. Perceval, in a suit from Savile Row but just a little baggy at the knees, had put aside the *Daily Worker* to read a novel of Kafka—in the original, of course.

CROWDER: Good Lord, there's Louis MacNeice.

PERCEVAL: I expected him.

CROWDER: Where's he going?

PERCEVAL: He's going to write a book.

CROWDER: Bad show, eh?

PERCEVAL: Bad show.

CROWDER: Bad form travelling with a kit bag.

PERCEVAL: Yes, he's pretending to be tough.

CROWDER: What's he writing a book about?

PERCEVAL: Islands. Very decadent.

CROWDER: Which islands? Do I know them?

PERCEVAL: No, of course you don't.

CROWDER: Oh, those ones!

Silence for five minutes. Perceval sniffs cocaine, Crowder cleans his pipe.

CROWDER: Tell you what!

PERCEVAL: Tell me what.

CROWDER: Let's go there too.

PERCEVAL: Where?

CROWDER: Islands.

PERCEVAL: Why?

CROWDER: Why not?

PERCEVAL: I don't know.

CROWDER: Done!

Another pause during which Perceval takes up his *Kafka* and Crowder fills his pipe with tobacco.

CROWDER: Hell of a lark, eh?

PERCEVAL: Why?

CROWDER: I don't know.

PERCEVAL: Perhaps you're right.

Crowder puts his pipe in his mouth, Perceval puts his *Kafka* on the seat.

CROWDER: So he's going to write a book about the islands?

PERCEVAL: Yes.

CROWDER: Let's write a book about *him.*

PERCEVAL: No.

CROWDER: Why?

PERCEVAL: My dear Crowder, I have never had time for minor cerebral exercises. I have never gone in for pelmanism, crossword puzzles or detective fiction. I have never kept a diary or written to the *Observer* to say when I first heard the cuckoo. And I am not at this time of my life going to start writing about that!

CROWDER: What?

PERCEVAL: Him.

CROWDER: Oh, him?

Pause. The train draws into a station. A lady and gentleman come in and ask if the two corner seats are occupied. I say 'No' and they sit down respectively on top of Crowder and Perceval.

CROWDER: What the hell!

PERCEVAL: What the hell indeed! She uses Quelques Fleurs.

CROWDER: I don't believe he saw us.

PERCEVAL: Oh, yes he did. He just said 'No' on purpose.

CROWDER: How can we take it out of him?

PERCEVAL: I know.

CROWDER: Who knows?

PERCEVAL: We'll write a book about him.

CROWDER: Oh, *you* know!

PERCEVAL: Yes, *him*!

CROWDER: When do we start?

PERCEVAL: We've started.

Perceval takes out his notebook, Crowder lights his pipe. The lady and gentleman move uncomfortably in their seats. The train draws into a tunnel.

II

JOURNAL: LONDON TO STORNOWAY

I HAD of course actually seen Crowder and Perceval, and it was in order to annoy them that I deliberately told the lady and gentleman that their seats were empty. I was, however, a little embarrassed to hear that they were going to trail me round the islands. There is no knowing what one may do on an island and it is an unpleasant thought to know that, whatever one does, Crowder and Perceval will be in on it. I would much rather have been accompanied by Anthony Blunt with whom I lately travelled in Spain, or by Wystan Auden with whom I lately travelled in Iceland. Both of these had commented on my going to the Hebrides.

'You seem to have a mania for going North,' Anthony Blunt had said.

Anthony Blunt is an art critic, ex-Cambridge don, with a passion for the Baroque. He thinks it odd to suffer discomfort when there are no *objects* to be seen for it. Nature is all very well, he would say, but is a bore when taken neat.

'One goes North,' Wystan Auden said to me, 'in order to escape from sex.' Just in the same way as one goes west in order to die—viz., Chicago.

Wystan Auden, as everyone should know, is a poet and English Eccentric. He would agree that nature in the nude is a bore. He likes the human element; his favourite landscape is the Black Country. He could not, however, object to my going North as it was he who persuaded me last summer to go to Iceland.

Before that I had been further North still—to Spitzbergen. There is little to be said for Spitzbergen except that it would do as a *décor* for the late F. H. Bradley's 'unearthly ballet of bloodless categories'. The highest vegetation on Spitzbergen is a lichen. Striped pyramids rise from the sea with glaciers between them. No one lives there except coal miners. The coal is inferior quality.

But the Hebrides seemed a different proposition. I put them in the Western category rather than the Northern. Death rather than sexlessness. I hoped to find them like the West of Ireland—a wild landscape and a genial people. I thought it would be a nice rest after London—London, where people keep asking one for lifts to Finsbury Park or to dramatise *Wuthering Heights*. Where tall women like Amazons walk into one's flat and throw over the tea-table. Where one's landlord puts in the lease that one must not have a dog or a cat over 21 pounds in weight. (When I wrote and told him I had a borzoi he generously made an exception.) London, where I permeate to work through traffic blocks only to be asked by intelligent German pupils on what system the English pronounce Greek.

On what system indeed? On what system do they pronounce Greek, Latin, French or English? On what system do they work, eat or enjoy themselves? The

English are devils for routine but system is beyond them. I will try the Scots, I said, and get some money in advance on them. But not the mainland Scots whom I know already. No, no, I said, I will go to the islands and recuperate from physical exhaustion.

But first of all I must get myself exhausted. That was easy. I went to Birmingham on March 18th and played rugger for the first time since 1926. I played against King Edward's Grammar School, Aston, as an honorary member of the Old Boys' team. I played centre three-quarter where I had never played in my life. My friends came to watch, thinking that I would be sick on the field. I borrowed boots two sizes too large and looked like Donald Duck. I was not sick on the field, but after the game I had brandy in the pavilion.

Now, I thought, I am entitled to a rest in the islands. I went to David Macbrayne, Ltd., in Cockspur Street and bought myself a highly complicated time-table. I knew hardly any of the names except Skye and I ruled out Skye at once (I know a red-headed Labour Party economist who went to Skye in shorts.) I looked further down the list and ruled out Iona for I remembered what Dr. Johnson had said, 'That man is little to be envied, whose patriotism would not gain force upon the plain of Marathon, or whose piety would not grow warmer among the ruins of Iona.' I had no wish to take a chance on this particular test of piety.

I bought a quarter-inch map which showed me Skye and the Outer Islands. I liked the look of Rhum, whose three glens meet in the centre, but was told it was forbidden country—a gamekeeper's desolation. Over Edom shall I cast out my fly, Moab and Kish shall be desolate and deer or grouse shall inhabit the land. In Dr. Johnson's time the island was inhabited by very small horses 'eminent for beauty' and by 'fifty-eight families, who continued Papists for some time after the Laird became a Protestant. Their adherence to their old religion was strengthened by the countenance of the Laird's sister, a zealous Romanist, till one Sunday, as they were going to Mass under the conduct of their patroness, MacLean met them on the way, gave one of them a blow on the head with a *yellow stick*, I suppose a cane, for which the *Earse* had no name, and drove them to the kirk, from which they have never since departed.'

Today was April 3rd and I had left Euston by the ten train for Edinburgh in which I now sat. I have always regarded Euston as the station for the North of Ireland, having many early memories of sitting on a tuck-box among its smells. I consider that the Great Hall has been spoiled since they substituted Information Bureaus for the series of glass cases containing models of trains. The trains lit up when you put in a penny and that is more than you can expect of an Information Bureau.

I had with me a very un-Hebridean book, *The Notebooks and Papers of Gerard Manley Hopkins*. I had a copy for review but ought to have foreseen that I should be unable to read it until I returned to London. It was very heavy. I took it out now, in order to impress Perceval, and went to sleep with it in my hand. I was very tired, having been up all night supervising a young Scotsman who had been typing out a play for me. His company had prepared me for the transition from England; he himself had spent two years as a farm-hand in Mull. The great event of the year in Mull, he told me, was the Peat Cutting.

I passed through beautiful Cumberland and tried to think that the Hebrides would be preferable. A ring of noisy foam, a welter of seals and black-haired Noble Celts. Like the first time I ever went to the West of Ireland. The first time I went to the West of Ireland I drove in a saloon car with my father, and as we came over a hill, still some miles from the coast, my father, who had not been back there for many years, leaped in his seat under the constricting roof and cried like Xenophon's troops 'The Sea! The Sea!' I looked over his shoulder and saw, where the land dipped far off, a regular leap of white like the flash of an animal's teeth. The seas there show their teeth continually. I thought the Scotch sea would be like that too. I had always been prejudiced against Scotland, having been there several times when a boy. A monotony of heather, a lack of the pleasant word: those were my two chief impressions. I had been to Edinburgh, Aberdeen, Inverness, but thought that the West would be different. A Scottish Nationalist, the December before last, had said to me on Prince's Street Station, waving a glass of brandy carried without spilling from the County Restaurant, 'You work a revolution in Ireland, and I will do the same in the Highlands: between us we will blot out the Low-lands of Scotland and Ulster.' So I took it that when I went in Scotland north and west I should find the same pleasant changes as when in Ireland going west and south. From degraded Ulster with its brooks running from the factories sulphur-yellow, stinking of chlorine, and its faces stiff with the fear of giving a point to anyone, to the faces that are able to smile and voices that give no headaches, white houses on patchwork-quilt hills and hedges of fuchsias.

In Edinburgh I met my friend Hector MacIver who is a Lewisman. We had many whiskies and ate a haggis to the strains of a light orchestra. The music annoyed Hector, who told me that negro spirituals were a crib from the Hebridean. Via Arkansas, he said. I did not believe this for a moment, but it reminded me that Paul Robeson likes the Hebridean melodies. (He sings Russian and Hebridean but draws the line at Lieder.) Hector told me I must start the Outer Islands from the north, not from the south. With great precision he mapped me out an itinerary. Hector is one of those good Scots who can be equally lyrical and practical. He told me with splendid venom how Lord Leverhulme had wanted to turn Lewis into a Port Sunlight, had failed, thanks to the noble obstinacy of the islanders, and in a fit of pique had sold off the island in blocks and very cheap to the ragtag and bobtail of England. And he told me how he himself as a boy had fooled a landlord. Hector was going by with his rods to poach salmon and the landlord sent the keeper after him to ask where he was going. So Hector said he was going to catch lobsters. The landlord on hearing that Hector was going to catch lobsters with a rod said, 'All the people are mad here', and stumped off in disgust.

'Debunk the landlords,' Hector said. 'Uncultured tyrants!' I said I would if I met any. As it turned out, I didn't on my first trip. On my second trip I saw one landlord in a kilt, with a dirk (technically, a skeandhu) tucked in his stocking. He is a sassenach who changed his name. In the Hebrides kilts are only worn by the immigrants. Most of the landlords anyway are bloodless abstractions—So-and-so Estates Limited.

I had to stay Sunday in Edinburgh. There was a heavy mist; the Castle Rock could not be seen from Prince's Street. I visited the National Gallery as I had last done on my way to Iceland. It is pleasing to have a hurried snatch of art on one's way into the wilderness. Like Marlene Dietrich in that film where she ran off into the desert in high-heeled shoes. There are a great many bad pictures in this gallery and a few lovely ones. The latter, however, seem a little out of place. For instance, Tiepolo's magnificent 'Finding of Moses', is too cultured in its aerial solidity to live beneath the crazy fir-cone of the Scott Memorial. And Dégas' portrait of Diego Martelli and Gauguin's 'Jacob Wrestling with the Angel' have a nervous and almost gay sophistication alien to this race of preachers and engineers. I noticed Perceval looking at the Tiepolo but Crowder was not to be seen. When I came out there was a crowd outside the building listening to a speaker on a box, a heavy crusader of the Craigavon build who was denouncing the Church of Rome as a crook commercial organisation—'When the Pope dies every Roman Catholic in the world has to pay two-and-six for prayers for his soul. *I know what kind of a soul he has.*'

I had to get up at 3.00 next morning to catch my train for Mallaig. I had been told that this was one of the two best scenery-runs in Scotland, if not in the British Isles. I cannot say that I greatly enjoyed it. From Glasgow to Mallaig is indeed almost a continuous stretch of what is called 'Scenery'. Scenery as distinct from landscape. While landscape is judged mainly by æsthetic criteria, the appeal of scenery is meretricious. With a Mayfair belle all that is demanded in the face is a few signpost details such as plucked eyebrows and lipstick—anything sufficiently artificial (stylized is the word preferred) to show that she knows the ropes. With scenery again all that is needed is certain inversions or distortions of the more usual features of landscape. What was horizontal must become vertical, grass must become heather, rocks should be laid on extravagantly. As with the lady's face the more useless the details the better. Eliminate all ploughed fields.

When I was a little boy I had a passion for the wild, the bleak and the difficult in scenery. This tuned in with my other passions for the antique, the fantastic, the war-like, the martyred and the Irish. All these perhaps could be subsumed under the last. I was brought up in a very prosaic context on the northern shore of Belfast Lough. Belfast does not offer much in the way of the antique, the wild or the fantastic, but this did not undermine my belief that these qualities were typical of a nation to which I was extremely proud to belong. I could always ignore the evidence around me on the ground that the real Irish lived in the South. The South, which I had never visited, had all the virtues of legend. I had the bad luck, I thought, to live among hybrid Ulster Scots but I myself was autochthonous, descended from an Irish king—the name MacNeice being derived from Conchubar MacNessa, the villain of the Deirdre saga. (In later years I was told that the derivation was much more probably from Naoise, the hero of the same saga, and since then I have, in defiance of natural history, claimed descent from both of them at once and in each case by Deirdre.) Being then autochthonous Irish and with a father who was at that time a Home Ruler I at an early age thought that it was my religious duty to be a rebel and that the best of all terms of reproach was the word 'English'. English meant everything that was flat, dull and unenterprising. English governesses had minds that never rose above keeping your hands clean and your feet dry; at the same time they had no bump of locality and could be kept walking in circles within a mile of home under the impression that they had gone four miles straight and had to come four miles back again. As for the English landscape—the word my father used for it was 'stodgy'. Looking out from a train at the sun on the newly green hawthorn hedges he would say, 'In England they would pay pounds to see that'. But he would suggest that the West of Ireland—*that* was the place for scenery: rocks, mountains, lakes, waterfalls and the sea. I correlated these pictures with Moore's Irish Melodies and thought of myself as an outlaw hiding in an amethyst mountain. Yet the wildest part of Ireland I had been to was for a long time Portstewart, the humbler sister of Portrush.

I digress a little further to speak of Portstewart because one's holiday experiences in childhood must, I feel, partly determine one's reactions to later holidays. I was taken to Portstewart about the age of five or six and did not visit it again till I was twenty when I went there to play golf with my father's curate. I was very astonished to see Portstewart again both because it was the same and because it was different. I remembered coming out of a station which was thoroughly inland; outside the station door was a bush of buddleia and my parents gave me some preserved ginger from a paper bag. I had no idea what was coming next. I walked along with my parents eating preserved ginger and suddenly—over a rise or round a corner—there came in my face a crash of salt and vitality, the wind blew over from the sea and the sea was unbelievably blue. We went further and there was a pier exuberantly smelling of fish. The fishermen were shaking out their nets, shining with fish and here and there a dead seagull. The gulls were thrown back into the water and the sight of them horrified me. (I had always thought of nets as evil because of an illustration in *The Pilgrim's Progress.*)

We stayed in lodgings on the sea-front where I drank so much milk that the landlady said she would need a cow. Along the front ran trams. Most of the time we collected shells—mainly limpets—but we also walked round the castle which stood on a wild promontory. This was vastly dangerous. A rock-path ran round the castle; the castle towered above us; below, far below, was the sea. The sea was never quiet; if we fell into it we should be smashed to pieces. One day I looked down from the cliff and there among the rocks were two bathers floating on wings. I was terrified and thought that they would be drowned.

I was also taken for a walk inland between high walls.

On the top of the walls grew long feathery grasses and the grass was whistling in the wind, blown out horizontal. I formed a picture of great space beyond those walls, tundras that never ended whipped by the salt wind. But most exciting of all was the golf-links. The golf-links lay along the river Bann. From the Bann projected odd-shaped waterworks and I thought of these as malevolent. Where we walked the grass was crisp and bouncy and occasionally, at huge intervals, we found a strange red flag. This flag had something to do with the waterworks.

When I came back with the curate we played golf and I had a feeling of blasphemy. For this which was once mystery, delight and terror was now only a matter of trying to do holes in bogey. And I realised also that now no visual objects ever struck me so vividly.

In going for a holiday I usually hope to recapture some of that vividness. If things are strange enough they are bound to shake you up. But the more obvious strangenesses do not function; they are something one has seen on the movies. I have no wish ever to go to the Alps. I still like what is bleak and comparatively desolate, was delighted by the country north-west of Madrid. But I only want the comparatively desolate; a complete lack of vegetable or animal life leads to anæsthesia. A few sheep scattered on the Wiltshire downs make the downs seem much more lonely. I am thinking of the loneliness which is attractive like melancholy music. Despair is, I suppose, something more melancholy still, but it seems better to make a rigorous distinction; melancholy and despair two things different in kind, melancholy being sometimes good and despair never so. In the same way there should be two names for loneliness, for the kind which is attractive if sentimentally so, and for the kind which approximates to nothingness. The lava-fields of Iceland cured me of the idea that a landscape cannot be too bleak. To appreciate even the stoniness of stones you need something else to set them off. The miles and miles of stones in Iceland had for me none of the stony charm of the rocks of Connemara which are broken by gorse or cottages.

In going to the Hebrides I hoped to find the right ratio of life and barrenness. People had told me that it would be very warm, that the sun would shine all day, that there would be many wild flowers catching the early spring. This was not quite what I wanted (I wanted foam and wind) but looking at the map I was reassured. Lewis and Harris, Uist and Barra, lie out there as outposts; beyond them America. Ergo, the full weight of the Atlantic must break upon them and over them. I remembered the island of Omey off County Galway where my father went looking for the house in which he had been born and found at last some stones on a small knoll near the west coast—no tree or rock to protect, the spray must have reached them from the ocean and the noise been always in their ears. An old barefoot woman had come up and said in a very broad brogue, 'You will be one of the MacNeices; I can see you know the lie of the ground.' (My father had not been there since he was nine.) Everyone had emigrated, she said, for the potatoes had ceased to grow—'If my mother was alive now, you could hear her crying all over the island.'

I was a little depressed to remember that the Scottish

islanders speak Gaelic. I am all in favour of their speaking Gaelic but I realised that their English talk would consequently not represent them. Hector MacIver had said that I must mix with the Gaelic-speaking population. But how to mix? I find it difficult enough to mix with the English-speaking population outside the very small clique in which talking and listening come natural to me. And there are two types of travellers whom I detest—the lovers of the quaint who patronise the natives and the plus-four wits who are facetious about them. I am almost bound to be one or other at moments in this book. Of enthusiasm applied from the outside I once met a good example in the person of a brewing lady—I mean the wife of a titled brewer. I met her once at tea. She was very large and wore a mushroom hat. Suddenly she leant over to me. 'Are you interested in the antiquities?' she said.

'What antiquities?'

'All of them.'

'Oh,' I said.

'It was the English,' she said, 'they drove them out.'

I left it at that but met her again at an Encaenia lunch-party in All Souls' at Oxford. 'It is beautiful here,' she said, 'so beautiful. These vistas, you know,' pointing at a blank wall. 'It is very reposeful.' I agreed. A friend of mine came up, spoke to me rapidly and incomprehensibly and went away again.

'What nationality is that young man?' she said.

'Jewish.'

'I thought so,' she said sinisterly.

'He's very clever,' I said, apologising.

'I know they are,' she said, 'but I can't see why they should be.'

I drew my gown about me and looked demurely on the ground. I was up against something impregnable.

When such people travel they are like the wooden horse that took Troy. Large, creaking, like nothing on earth in nature, they are let within the walls. Then up comes the great trap-door of their mouth and out pop the armed platitudes, the ready-made gushing eulogies, picking on the picturesque and spearing anything that is quaint. Later comes the army of trippers, the alien rank and file.

At Mallaig I took the boat to Kyle of Lochalsh and at Kyle another boat for Stornoway, where I arrived about nine in the evening. The boat was a babel of Gaelic which sent me comfortably to sleep. A great crowd came down to meet the boat, as is their custom, and I shambled along dimly-lit quays to an hotel, having a pleasant feeling of unreality between the grey houses and the water streaked with reflections. I did not want a meal in the hotel, so went to a fish restaurant. Here there was an angry scene. A group of fishermen, speaking in English, began to malign the English. A young man sitting behind me with a friend took offence at this. He had a yellow pullover, a cloth cap and a face which was amiable if unfinished. He said that his old man was English and as good as any bloody person there. The other group got angry in their turn. 'We have to take it in England,' they said, 'so they can bloody well take it here.' The young man, very red in the face and rather drunk, jumped up but was pulled down in his chair by his friend. The proprietor, a masterly man who looked as if he had Italian blood in him, came in and spoke with authority, 'You get on and eat your —— fish dinner.' The anti-English group suggested that the young man should take a walk with them outside. 'You guys shut up,' said the proprietor, turning on them. He then solved the situation by expelling the minority. The majority wanted to follow the young man and beat him up but the proprietor quelled them. 'You guys!' he said ferociously. I poured tomato sauce over my fish and chips and found it excellent.

Stornoway I find a very exciting name. Scandinavian, as are most of the names in the islands. A suggestion of remoteness and adventure which was borne out by the scene in the fish restaurant. The islands are going to be lively, I decided. I walked home along the quiet quay where the fishing boats lay against the herring season, many of them with oddly gentle names—*Celandine, Sweet Promise, Verbena, Virtue and Dove.*

III

DIALOGUE IN STORNOWAY

(In the lounge of an hotel. My head is in the air. My foot is on the floor. They look at each other for some time before they speak.)

FOOT: Qu'allez-vous faire dans cette galère?
HEAD: Just a spot of belles-lettres, my dear.
Messrs. Longman and Curtis Brown
Are standing treat to the folks in town.
You have no idea how the cockney public
Is fetched by people who talk in Gaelic.
FOOT: But you don't know any Gaelic yourself.
HEAD: All my Gaelic lives on the shelf
Along with my Basque, my Breton and Manx;
I haven't time for linguistic pranks.
I see you are wearing the suit I said.
FOOT: I am wearing my brown with rubbers, Head.
A Moorish bootblack with much éclat
Nailed them on in the Alcalá.
I rather fancy a mustard bath.
HEAD: Are you forgetting the pilgrim's path?
It's axiomatic: when Grub Street goes
Into the wilds, it has to pose,
Wear leather elbows and thick-ribbed socks

And bark its shins on chosen rocks
And be punctuated with stings like commas
From fleas the size of Bristol Bombers,
Sleep in damp beds and eat half-cooked
Meals and be made a fool and rooked
And miss connections and lose its purse
And beautifully go from bad to worse——
At the end of which its Grub Street desk
Is simply littered with the picturesque.

FOOT: And you will be flattered for your style
But I shall be merely paid by the mile.

HEAD: Well, that is the way things are you know.

FOOT: That I should be billed as a gigolo!
I have a good mind to take to drink.

HEAD: Those who walk don't have to think.

FOOT: And those who think don't have to walk,
All they do is talk and talk
And who is any the better for that?
The gutter-sparrow and the alley-cat
Are just as chatty and more expressive——

HEAD: My dear, I think you had better undress if
You want to wake up fit for the fray.
Tomorrow, remember, is another day.

FOOT: What always riles me is the——
That is talked by intellectuals.
With a clipped accent and a market name
They utter clichés just the same.
Now we have reached these blessed islands
What do you say to a little silence?

HEAD: Oh no, my little philistine,
(I call you little though your size is nine)

You won't get any silence from me,
These blessed islands are my cup of tea.
It's partly, I suppose, the time of year——
I'm the only person like me round here.

FOOT: I'll say you are but I've no doubt
There are lots of chaps like me about.

HEAD: But not so many in the lucky station
Of having a boss with imagination.
Though I shall plot and shape the whole
Yours will be yet a useful role;
Before you lie imposing vistas——

FOOT: Calluses, impetigo and blisters.
I know your sense of humour, Head.
Who is it takes the top of the bed?

HEAD: But the hot bottle is yours, my dear.

FOOT: There's no great hope of a bottle here.

HEAD: I'll have to say what I've said before,
I fear you are lacking in *esprit de corps*.

FOOT: And may I point out—or is that unfair?——
That you are continually up in the air?

HEAD: I find your brand of humour low,
It's not even good of its kind, you know.

FOOT: Yes, you make me darn well laugh.
Nibbling the tree-tops like a giraffe——

HEAD: I suppose you think it a sign of blue blood
To be always groping around in the mud.

FOOT: And what is more, I consider it rude
The way you go out and about in the nude.
I always wear my suit of leather
And underclothes the colour of heather,
But how can you hope to inspire respect

In me for you as one of the elect
If when you go out, you leave behind
Your Homburg suit which is so refined?
How can you fancy folk in the street
Will think that *you* are one of the élite?

HEAD: Force of character will carry me through
And that will never be said of you——
You ninny, you, you automaton,
You Never-Was, you As-Good-As-Gone!

FOOT: I'll make you eat your words, I'll take
My leave and begone for good; you fake.

HEAD: Go on and try, go on and try.

FOOT: I'll break away from you or die.

HEAD: How are you going to cross the Minch?
Why, you couldn't——

FOOT: The rhyme is inch.
I always know what you're going to say,
I'm just as bright as you any day.

HEAD: Oh you think you're bright? Well, prove it,
Take your precious self and move it.

FOOT: Here goes now.

HEAD: Where goes?

FOOT: There.
There, I've moved. Look, I'm here.

HEAD: But that's exactly where you were.

FOOT: No, I wasn't.

HEAD: Yes, you were.
You were there.

FOOT: I was not.
I was there.

HEAD: Well, mark the spot,

You go back and show me where.
FOOT: Can't be bothered to go back there.
HEAD: Well, why not try going out of the door?
FOOT: Oh, I think that would be rather a bore.
Now I've proved my point to you
That I can do just what I want to do,
I think I'll take a bit of a nap.
HEAD: Oh, you think you will, old chap?
Well, think again. I feel on the whole
There still is time for an evening stroll,
And I think it might seem rather unkind
To take the air and leave you behind;
You can have your nap a little later——
You holy fraud, you second-rater,
You who think you can take your ease
Now you've got to the Hebrides.
You've got another think coming to you,
I'll make you walk till all is blue
And more than walk before I've done——
Get up, you lazy bastard, RUN.

IV

JOURNAL: NESS, SHAWBOST AND UIG

THE main part of Stornoway lies on a peninsula. On three sides are quays. My hotel was in Cromwell Street and looked across the narrow tongue of the harbour to the wooded grounds of Stornoway Castle which are now known as Lady Lever Park. The trees in the park are almost the only trees on Lewis. In Stornoway Castle, a huge castellated building in the Scotch Baronial style, Lord Leverhulme, I was told, used to sleep in a room in the tower with a bath alongside his bed and no roof above him. When he left Lewis because the people were unsympathetic towards his plans, he gave the Parish of Stornoway to the people. The castle has proved an encumbrance. In the summer they attempt to lease it to English grandees. The alternative plan which some have suggested, is to take off the roof.

Lady Lever Park with its fir trees and fly-blown rhododendrons might be anywhere. There is nothing Hebridean about it or even Scottish. Just inside the grounds is a placard nailed to a tree—

'Save Money by Spending Wisely. Salads in Season. Fresh Flowers. Daily Wreaths Crosses Bouquets. At Reasonable Prices.'

In Stornoway I went to see the editor of the *Stornoway Gazette*. The *Stornoway Gazette* comes out once a week and its most popular page is entitled 'Where your friends are sailing'—particulars concerning about two hundred sailing vessels which have Lewismen on board. The great career in the Hebrides is the dole but the merchant service comes second. Many of the merchant sailors manage to come home every so often and get their share of the dole also. The editor told me that he was collecting statistics about emigration which in late years had ceased but which in the three years after the war had drained off about three thousand young Lewismen—almost a whole generation. This, he said, was one of the reasons why religion in Lewis had become narrower and inferior, the young were not there to vivify and modify. A Lewisman, who is now a minister in Ontario, had written a book entitled *May Sabbath-keeping Prevent Church-going?* including arguments based on the book of Exodus as to whether a man who lives beyond walking distance from a church is entitled to go to church by bus.

Fish and tweed are the chief businesses of Stornoway. Lately there has been a big change in the method of tweed manufacture. Very few crofters now do the whole thing themselves—spinning, dyeing and weaving; most of them weave it for the mills who issue them the wool ready spun. An old lady in Lewis showed me a shawl which her mother had made entirely with her own hands from the wool of her own sheep. This idyllic if laborious self-sufficiency has now been nearly eliminated by modern specialisation.

Mr. Grant, the editor, told me that the most important

date in the recent history of Lewis was the passing of the Crofters' Act in 1876, which precluded the danger of wanton eviction and spiked the guns of wicked factors such as the notorious Donald Munro who used to stride through the land, saying 'I'll have the croft off ye'. The crofters nowadays have even the right to be articulate and come up to Stornoway to plead for themselves in the Land Court where a Gaelic interpreter is always in attendance because, though the crofters usually know English, they find it easier to be litigious in Gaelic. Two crofters recently walked twelve miles to the Court for the sake of a shilling or rather for the sake of a principle; they thought that they were being excluded from their immemorial grazing rights on a small island. They lost their case and had to pay £2 12*s.* 6*d.* expenses.

Stornoway parish is now self governing, the land having been given to the people by Lord Leverhulme. Ten trustees are popularly elected but the scheme so far has not worked altogether happily. Mr. Compton Mackenzie would no doubt say that this was the fault of the west wind (see page 99). Mr. Grant tended to think that there was something to be said for the pre-Leverhulme days of landlords who were semi-feudal, benevolent despots. Benevolent because themselves islanders.

As for the herring-fishery, Mr. Grant told me that Stornoway was badly affected by Prohibition in America. The Stornoway herring is exceptionally large and tasty and the Americans, being connoisseurs in this matter, used to import large quantities of these herrings, salted, for use in their saloons—the salted Stornoway herring being a great thirst-maker. Mr. Grant also lamented that

Lewis did not grow her mutton for export for the Lewis mutton is, he says, better than any mutton in the Highlands, while any mutton in the Highlands is, as everyone knows, better than any mutton in the Lowlands—'The mountain sheep are sweeter.'

The *Stornoway Gazette* is a paper which travels the world. In the Argentine there is a ranch of Lewismen who read it two months old and 'phone the contents to their friends in the backwoods. I found it odd to think of that presbyterian (Free Church probably) oasis among the pampas.

It is to be regretted that the *Stornoway Gazette* which is the only paper published in the islands, should be almost entirely in English. The editor, a charming young man, believes in progress and no doubt thinks that an English paper is more progressive. Not far from his office is a large building which includes the Town Hall and the Public Library. In the latter the Gaelic-speaking population are treated to the *Tatler* and the *Sketch* and the *Cornhill Magazine*.

Leaving Mr. Grant I went down to the quiet quay where a boat was unloading hay. Stornoway in April was quiet. It reminded me of little towns in the North of Ireland, the same streets of grey cemented houses, the same slummy smell, the same sombre women hurrying by the wall in shawls. I passed a church which had been turned into a tweed depot and the Town Council Chambers, a repellent turreted building of heather-purple stone with brown facings to the windows. I thought that the sooner I got out of this town the better, but the Scots have no sense of time and could not tell me when the bus left. (In Stornoway by the way everyone, as a young man pointed out to me at breakfast, gets up very late. There is no reason for them to get up earlier.) At last in the late afternoon I got the bus to Ness. The buses are uncomfortable and crowded and carry more chattels than people. Their drivers are charming.

Just outside the town I saw some gorse. I did not realise at the time that either trees or gorse were rarities. The bus took me to Barvas where it followed the road to the right, i.e., to the North. From this point on I noticed the Black Houses. It was some time before I realised that the Black Houses are for people to live in. They grow out of the ground among and in the same way as peatstacks and haystacks, as dank-looking and nearly as windowless, and often not aligned with the road. Some of them look like very derelict Noah's Arks riding on the undulating boglands. They crawl up and downhill like tanks but the byre, through which the living-room is entered, is always at the lower end of the slope so that the stale of the cattle will not enter the living-room. The walls are often four feet thick, made of large stones without cement. I looked forward to entering one of these houses. The stretch of country from Barvas to Ness I found highly attractive though the islanders apologise for its monotony. It has no hills, which is a good thing, for a single jutting hill would spoil the magnificent stretch of bogs that go on and on, the colour of grizzly bears or burnt toast.

I asked to be let down at Cross where I wanted to see the schoolmaster. Unfortunately Cross is a village all length and no width and I had to leave my bags on the

Black House in Lewis. Exterior.

grass by the roadside and walk some distance back to the Schoolhouse. The schoolmaster was a typical Lewisman, large, silent and melancholy. His wife very hospitably gave me some tea and something to eat and I asked her husband where I could stay the night. He seemed to think it very improbable that I could stay anywhere but at last suggested a house someway back along the road to Barvas. I said that I had left my bags along the road in the other direction and asked if I could borrow a wheelbarrow to fetch them in. The wife said that she had a wheelbarrow, but the husband was very upset by the suggestion and finally allowed me to fetch my bags in it only on condition that he did not accompany me. It was pointed out to me that I should be a laughing-stock to the little boys of the village. I braved this and fetched my bags in the twilight, exhilarated by the noise of the barrow on the road.

I pass over the following night which was my most uncomfortable night in the Hebrides. My bed was damp and the sheets were not clean. The wallpaper was peeling from the walls. The house, as my hostess said, had fallen on evil days. I thought it very hospitable of her to take me in at all.

The sun shone next morning when I set out to walk to Lionel, where Hector had told me to see another schoolmaster. (Schoolmasters are the medicine-men of these islands.) From North Dell where I had stayed the night to the Port of Ness (between two to three miles) the road is one continuous village though it goes by different names—Cross, Suainabost, Habost and Lionel. (Names ending in *bost* are Norse; bost means 'steading'.) This must be a cheerful road to walk if you know enough people to drop in on. About half the houses seemed to be Black Houses and one in every three sheep to be a black sheep. The sheep are small and sturdy. The men working in the fields (not that there were many of these) wore calico shirts and sometimes trousers of an astonishingly gay blue colour, a warm blue, evidently a home-made dye. Outside the houses sat children and collie-dogs. The collies here are as collies should be, with round heads, intelligent and affectionate; most of them are black and white. Unlike the collies in Ireland they do not bark at strangers but are promiscuously friendly like the dogs of Iceland. One young dog I saw running round on three legs with one paw put through its collar; this was to stop it chasing sheep.

Scottish dogs I find on the whole regrettable. The show collie is an abomination and for a *multum in parvo* of irritation it is hard to beat a cairn. I have nothing to say for dandies or West Highland Whites while the Scottish deerhound looks sadly snipy if you compare him with an Irish wolfhound. The Scottish terrier is the best of the bunch but there is a woman whom I know who has two Scottish terrier bitches which have grown like her in character. She lives in a house full of mirrors set cunningly at angles so that while sitting in one room she can see what happens in another (no door is ever shut for she has claustrophobia); the two dogs lie at her feet looking down their long witch-like noses, their coats untrimmed, their claws scratching the matting. The memory of these sinister animals has set me against the breed.

I saw the schoolmaster at Lionel. His school is the largest in the island after Stornoway, and he himself is solidly and stolidly in keeping with it. He was very eager that I should walk up to the Butt of Ness to see the lighthouse. I thought that I would rather see Miss Kitty MacLeod, the Gaelic singer, at Skegersta. So I walked a good two miles south-east to Skegersta school-house where I saw Kitty MacLeod's mother, who instructed one of her pupils, aged about seven, to show me the way to their dwelling house. This little girl who had not yet learned her English, had a brown donkey-mop of hair and walked straight ahead like a donkey not looking to right or to left. Kitty MacLeod and her father received me hospitably and gave me a glass of milk warm from the cow and a couple of slices of bread. The father was sitting by a large open hearth in the kitchen tapping the floor with a stick. His daughter was very tired; back from her studies in Edinburgh she had spent the morning planting potatoes. While a charming short-haired white cat played around the kitchen she played me records of her own songs—a sea-song, unaccompanied, about a ship leaving Islay and an example of the old 'mouth-music'—Port-a-Beul—to which the islanders used to dance before they had musical instruments. Then she herself sang a very attractive cradle song. Mr. MacLeod tapped the floor with his stick and said that the world had changed for the worse; no one nowadays thought of anything but self.

From Skegersta I walked to the Port of Ness and there got a bus for Barvas. At Barvas I had tea in a house which used to be an inn but is now without a licence; there are no licensed houses down the west side of Lewis. From Barvas I got a lift on a doctor's car to Shawbost, passing through stony Bragair. The name Shawbost means the Steading by the Sea. Three roads run off at right-angles on the seaward side of the main road and end in blind alleys. Each of these roads is lined with a straggle of houses, many of them Black Houses. Shawbost has been described as follows by one of its natives, my friend Hector MacIver—'The village was bounded on the east and west by two huge headlands that flung themselves into the Atlantic like two crouching beasts cooling their dark bellies in the sea. The wide and shelterless bay that lay below the crofts was cleft by a long skerry at whose outermost end a rounded bastion of rock stood up above the stones. Where the tide flowed in over the skerry, this thing looked like the citadel of a drowning city over whose roofs the water was beginning to rise. To the south we were guarded by a ridge of high hills, and from the moors behind them the night leapt upon us in the winter-time with the suddenness of an animal's leap. The village was built for the most part on the two rocky ridges that rose gradually from the high valley which separated them . . . ' I hope Hector will forgive me if I say that Shawbost did not look at all like this to me. I missed the two rocky ridges and must have greatly under-estimated the two huge dark-bellied crouching head-lands. Part of the charm of Shawbost seemed to me to lie in the fact that there was nothing enormous or violent in its vicinity. But I have no doubt that in winter the sea can supply violence and that to Hector in his childhood the contours of the land seemed enormous.

Shawbost is a weaving centre. As you walk down the rugged road between the Black Houses your ears run the gauntlet of the shuttles. The steel looms have now for the most part supplanted the wood. The wooden loom gives a thicker cloth but produces, at its best, only half the cloth in the time.

After supper I walked back along the Barvas road to Bragair, where a son of my host is headmaster of the school. All the houses here have splendid fires of peat. They told me proudly that what you want is real black peat, not the white-fibred sort which gives no warmth. There are one hundred and twenty children in the Bragair school. Much of their work is done in Gaelic. Thirty years ago a child was slapped who spoke Gaelic in a Hebridean school. The young headmaster had been reading (and admiring) Liam O'Flaherty's *Spring Sowing*. It was significant, I thought, that he found it sympathetic for this northern part of Lewis is in many ways reminiscent of Ireland. The chief difference is that the Black Houses of Lewis are black while the Irish cottages liven the landscape with their whiteness.

On the next day there was a country wedding in Shawbost. During the morning little boys ran along the route of the procession sticking up improvised flags on the earthern dykes—white shirts or handkerchiefs on bamboo poles. I walked with my host to the shore about half a mile north of his house; in the winter storms the spray blows over to his house. On the shore was a large heap of wrack rotting into beautiful manure. As we approached it exploded in a cloud of starlings and blackbirds who were rummaging the wrack for worms. My host told me that dulse is eaten here and that the coast is a good ground for lobsters and crabs. The lobsters are sent to London but the crabs won't live that distance. On return from my walk I went into a Black House, the only one in the district which still has a circular fire. The fire is in the middle of the room on the hard-baked earthen floor, the room is warm and animal but not malodorous. This is true of even those houses which are full of animals and I fancy that the peat-smell may counteract the other smells. The lady of the house, a good-humoured if somewhat simple-minded old woman, apologised that her box-bed had not been made for sometime.

The Black Houses of Lewis are represented in the illustration on page 47. The old woman who had the central fire, shown opposite, was delighted to be drawn,

Black House, Interior, showing central fire.

and said, 'You can see that's me—the way I put my hand to my face.' Her house contains only one room other than the byre and here is an inventory of her furniture:

A box-bed with a curtain round the bottom of a cretonne patterned with pink roses.

A wooden bench that would seat four persons, fixed to the wall.

A dresser.

A three-legged stool.

A box used as a table; on the box is propped a flimsy little bookshelf containing broken mirror sets. A chest covered with a piece of stuff.

One picture and one calendar.

Two oil-lamps.

Some hens.

There is no table and no chair. The floor is of beaten earth rising in the middle where the fire is made.

The walls (presumably of mud) are covered with a striped rose-patterned wallpaper, very much discoloured with smoke, and the same wallpaper covers the dresser and the ceiling. The room is lit (but to no great extent) by a small slat of glass let into the roof.

In the afternoon I felt unwell which was a pity as I had hoped to wangle an invitation to the wedding party in the evening. The nearest doctor was seven miles away. I thought of walking to him but it began to rain. The Black Houses in the rain looked like covered barges. No Black House proper has a gable or eaves, the roof is rounded at each end and instead of the roof projecting from the wall the wall projects from the roof. The walls are four or five feet thick and the windows are either small panes let into the bottom of the thatch or else small panes sunk in a four-foot hole in the walls. I (lapsing for once into the romantic tripper) thought that it would be very nice to live in a house like this all among one's children and animals; one would lose the distinctions of species.

I felt too unwell to bother about the wedding reception which went on all night till six in the morning. Next morning I was due to move on to Valtos but after breakfast I was given a rug and lay on the sofa and groaned. As I lay by myself looking into the peat-fire, I heard voices behind me. I did not turn round for I knew too well whose they were—

CROWDER: The sissy! Now we'll have to wait till he gets well.

PERCEVAL: He probably won't get well.

CROWDER: Oh, yes, he will. Just introduce him to Dona Cascara Sagrada.

PERCEVAL: I find this country of exceedingly little interest.

CROWDER: All right if one had a gun.

PERCEVAL: I should say it's neurotic.

CROWDER: What is?

PERCEVAL: MacNeice's complaint.

CROWDER: Shall I put that in my notebook?

PERCEVAL: No. There's no point in putting down truisms.

CROWDER: Lord, I'm bored.

PERCEVAL: Well, sing us an Auld Scots Song.

CROWDER: Sang you mean.

PERCEVAL: Sang I mean.

CROWDER: I don't know any Auld Scots Sangs.

PERCEVAL: Then make one up.

CROWDER: I can't. I don't know the lingo.

PERCEVAL: Don't mind about that. It's a matter of mood and cadence.

CROWDER: All right. I'll sing you a love-song.

(He sings)

Hey, my love, my sorrow,
  What'll ye do without me?
I'm leaving town tomorrow,
  I won't come back, I doubt me.
Your face will fall a yard,
  Your stocks will fall to zero.
You'll find it awful hard
  When I am gone, my dear-O.

Often you donned your silk,
  Followed me where I led,
You went home with the milk
  And I went home with a head.
The Mystery Tour's no more,
  No more the Night Excursion;
You'll have to take the floor
  With Down-in-the-Mouth MacPherson.

I gave ye button earrings,
  My nose was like a beagle's
To find my little dearing
  A present from Gleneagles;
Presents lined your path,
  Their price beneath enquiry,
Bath salts for your bath
  And entries for your diary.

All your thought was I,
I was all your notion,
You were all my eye
And now I need some lotion.
London calls tomorrow
Where folks will flock about me;
Hey, my love, my sorrow,
What'll ye do without me?

(proudly) What do you think of that?

PERCEVAL: Derivative, my dear, derivative.

CROWDER: How do you mean derivative?

PERCEVAL: And another point. A love song ought not to be satirical. That is just an affectation—the sort of thing people did in the nineteen-twenties. A love song must be a hundred per cent genuine. Otherwise it is boring.

CROWDER: By Jove, I've had an idea.

PERCEVAL: Really?

CROWDER: Let's call the doctor for MacNeice. Then we may be able to get a move on.

My heart warmed to Crowder as he said this and I turned to look at him, but he was already gone. A quick man off the mark. Perceval sat down by the fire and took a sniff of cocaine. Perceval and I by tacit convention looked through each other.

The doctor came and not only doctored me but gave me a lift on my way. He not only gave me a lift but stopped to show me a sight—the druidic stones of Callernish. I staggered out of his car, seedy to the power of *n*, and looked at the stones through a mist of pain and rain. They were very much what I expected. But they seemed all right of their kind. It is a pity when druidic stones are too finished, as they are at Stonehenge, just as it is a pity when Irish round towers become over-slender and aspire to frills. The nicest circle of stones I know is the Roll-Right Stones on the Cotswolds. These are all shorter than you are yourself and when you notice them you merely feel as if you had broken in on a picnic party. I cannot see why the druids built the Roll-Right Stones as they seem very out of keeping with their usual ostentation. The most ostentatious circle is of course Avebury which I used to bicycle to from school. The Avebury circle was so large that modern man tactlessly built a village in the middle. As for Stonehenge—

As for Stonehenge I have seen it only once. I had been having tea at Sherborne in Dorset with my old preparatory schoolmaster, Littleton Charles Powys, brother of John Cowper, T.F., and of other eminent Powyses. He told me I must certainly drive back via Stonehenge. The last time he had been there he had been with John Cowper, and J.C. had put his 'shaggy old head' in a pool of water on the altar stone and worshipped. I was so stirred by Littleton Powys' enthusiasm that I drove my car at sixty m.p.h. to Stonehenge to see if I should be moved to worship also. I was not. Looking across the downs I saw them black with cars and in the middle a set of child's toy bricks. Coming nearer I found that the bricks were surrounded by barbed wire and garrisoned by A.A. men. One had to pay for entry and enter through a stile worked by a slot machine. The man I was with found it extremely funny as we tried to picture John Cowper Powys putting his head on the altar stone. We decided that it would be a very good joke to give a party one night and come to Stonehenge and break it up. Though perhaps Perceval would say that that smacked of the nineteen-twenties.

The Callernish stones are said by tradition to be giants petrified by magic. The magic must have caught them in the midst of a most intricate manœuvre, but a manœuvre not of war but of recreation. It is pleasant to think that the giants who feature in literature as louts, should have practised the equivalent of morris-dancing. I cannot bear morris-dancing but it must have been a step up for the giants. Bad luck to be turned to stone in the middle of the figure.

I took a bus from Garynahine to Miavaig. It was cold in the bus and there was little knee-space. Most of the way my teeth chattered like a machine-gun. Every now and again the bus would stop and someone would very slowly cross a burn by stepping-stones or make his way through a gate. The islanders are astonishingly slow in their movements. Even the young men of twenty move as if they were eighty. By this stage I had such abdominal pains that I had ceased to notice the landscape or the coming of night. I was let down in the night at Miavaig. An apocalyptic figure jumped out of the ground and said, 'Have you come to see Mrs. G.?' I was too tired to be alarmed or even surprised by his abruptness. We entered a beautifully warm kitchen and Mrs. G., horrified by the clacking of my jaw, produced a basin of warm water for my feet. She lit yet another peat-fire in the parlour. All I wanted was to get to bed. I went up to my bedroom and was sick, then went to bed cursing the climate of Lewis. It is a muggy climate and undermines the systems of innocent strangers. Anyone who comes to Lewis should live on Eno's Fruit Salts. It is one of the cruellest jokes in geography that islands in the position of the Hebrides should be so much the opposite of bracing. I lay like a corpse under a portly oil-lamp and longed for my flat in Hampstead, my curtains in peach-coloured chintz with white Victorian bows and my borzoi sleeping on the sofa.

V

JOURNAL: HARRIS AND NORTH UIST

FOR a whole day in Miavaig I lay and groaned on my bed. The picturesque bay outside the window failed to delight me and I could not eat my meals although they were the best-cooked meals I had yet seen in the island. I lay weakly on my back and cursed everything Scottish. I deplored once more that my name began with Mac. I remembered how unhappy I had been in my 'teens driving through Scotland with my family—heather, heather, Scotch broth and heather—my stepmother waking me whenever I was falling asleep with an ardent demand that I look at the wonderful scenery.

Framed in the bedroom window some women were collecting sea-weed. They fastened it into a huge ring and a boat came and towed it across the bay. Later there was an enormous rainbow straddling the tiny bay with a Moorish arch. In the evening I felt not quite so ill and agreed to my hostess' suggestion that I should play chess with the apocalyptic figure of yesterday, a fierce old man in a sailor's jersey. His hair was cropped like a convict and he had the abrupt eye of an eagle.

He won the first game by sweeping his queen over the heads of her pawns and checking me. I felt that it was not etiquette to query this. The second game was more

Chess in Uig

prolonged. Every now and then the old man would jump up abruptly and pull down the blind. The blind would snap up and he would sit down. He would then move one of my knights and I would protest. We took each other's queens. The old man jumped up and pulled down the blind. 'How is Gower Street now?' he said. Again he tried to move my knight and again I protested. He jumped up with a jerk and pointed at a hanging on the wall. 'That came from Honolulu,' he said and sat down with a jerk. I won this game.

There is a Gaelic bridal song about Miavaig translated into English in the metre of the original by Hector MacIver—

I'd sail with you to Miavaig in Uig,
Even tho' in twilight, even tho' in twilight.
I'd sail with you to Miavaig in Uig,
Even thro' the dark and the sea-mist.

How shall we fare when the wind's in the sail
And storm-clouds gather, storm-clouds gather?
How shall we fare in the whirl of the gale,
Out in the midst of the Islands?

Morag bheag of the golden hair,
Fair as the dawning, fair as the dawning,
Morag bheag of the golden hair,
Lightly she stepped to her bridal.

Who is the maiden who dances with joy,
Like foam on the wave-tops, foam on the wave-tops?
Who is the maid on the dancing floor?
She is the bride who came sailing.

The next day was Sunday and I returned to the light of day. I went for a walk in the morning round the Valtos peninsula, thus meeting the whole population on their way to the Miavaig church. It seemed extraordinary that such a crowd should emerge from the few scattered houses on the hills. (This peninsula gives the effect of hills though it is marked green on the map.) The church-goers marched past me, wooden and black, like robots, and I went on to Reef, a very picturesque little clump of Black Houses and thence by a sheeptrack to Valtos, resting on the way in a bunker of silver sand. The sun shone for once and my road was many-coloured. At Valtos I called on a friend of Hector MacIver's, an out-of-work engineer from Edinburgh who plays on the fiddle. He gave me a glass of milk and some dry bread and told me that Valtos was not what it used to be as a port. Like many of the islanders he speaks slowly and sadly and his face is set in a fatalistic melancholy. He accompanied me to the top of the brae and said he was very sorry that I could not stay with him. I hurried home through Clibh (pronounced Cliff) and found myself about an hour late for lunch. This, however, caused little surprise or chagrin. The Scots have no sense of time.

During the afternoon I looked at some very odd books of popular religion. On the wall was a picture of a girl in pseudo-classic draperies and with Joan Blondell eyes entitled, 'Nearer to Thee'. I reflected that the parlours of the Hebrides could stock all the fun-fairs in the world with vases and bijoux to be won by throwing darts or hooplas or rolling balls into holes. They are also a place to go for clocks with eccentric chimes.

On Monday I felt very weak. I decided to shake off the dust of Lewis and go into Harris. To get from Uig to Harris by bus I should have had to go all the way by bus to Stornoway and thence take another bus south to Tarbert. I decided instead that I would walk through the mountains. I took the early morning bus to the hairpin bend in the road near Loch Morsgail and walked up a private road between rhododendrons to the loch. The shooting lodge looked very comfortable. This was one of Lord Leverhulme's shooting lodges. I remembered a man I knew at Oxford who was reputed to own half the Hebrides. No doubt he lived in places like this lodge with lovely comfortable armchairs and up-to-date radiators. A

Lewisman told me of this young man, that he went to fish one day and caught a six-inch trout. He took it in triumph to the village pub and said, 'Cook me this'—an action which horrified the natives who all decided he was mad.

A track leads south from Loch Morsgail into the hills. The hills today were monotonous, lacking in drama. There was no wild life, barring two pheasants, and no flowers. In England they told me that I should find the Hebrides full of precocious flowers. This was a lie. Later in the year monotonous brown will turn to monotonous purple. I sat on a flat stone and ate an apple. I had no other food with me and had about fifteen miles in front of me before reaching a civilised road. A little further on my track faded to nothing. I had been told to keep my eyes on a gap in the mountains. This proved a very uncertain guide and I wasted much time floundering in marshy ground and jumping over rivulets.

As I floundered and jumped I thought about Second Sight. Second Sight still flourishes in the Hebrides. The best authenticated story I know of it is the following (in which I have changed the names as the man who saw the vision is still young and alive).

The houses in the village were scattered at intervals along a road stretching towards the sea but ending in a blind alley some way short of it. One winter towards the end of the Great War, John —— was returning home from a ceilidh at two in the morning, walking in the direction of the sea, when he saw a great glow of light coming down the road towards him at the rate of about forty miles an hour. In the middle of the glow was a man without a head and with only one arm, moving effortlessly forward as if he were skating. When he came level with the Hopper's house he turned sharp at right angles and shot through the gate like an arrow.

John was so terrified that he dared not go past the Hopper's house, so he took a long detour through the bogs to reach his own house, which was fifty yards further down the road. When he got inside the door he fainted, as was recorded next morning by his family. Next day, which was a Wednesday, John's adventure was the talk of the village.

During the night following a Norwegian boat with a cargo of combustible chemicals ran on the rocks beyond the village and was blown to pieces. On Thursday morning all the villagers went out to look for the bodies but none could be found till John and another man came across one in a crevice in the rocks. It was headless and had only one arm. 'That,' said John, 'is the man I saw in the night.'

It was the only body found. As the war was on, timber was scarce for coffins, so they buried him in a large wooden box which they found in the Hopper's outhouse. That was why he had gone in at the Hopper's gate. He was looking for his own coffin.

Revolving this tale I went on floundering and jumping. After some time when I was getting hot and cross and seemed to have made very little progress, I noticed at some distance below me to my right a loch unlike any other lochs. I put on my glasses and saw that it was fringed with sea-weed. It was the fag-end of Loch Resort. I studied my map and found that there were three glens, each leading up to a loch in the mountains and with a river flowing down from the loch. I found a river and followed it hoping it was the right one. It was a very attractive river, narrow and deep, but I wasted much time following its windings.

The loch proved to be the right one, i.e., Loch Voshimid, as at the far end of it I found a well-made track leading south through the glen and at the head of the track a wooden shelter. I searched the shelter in case anyone should have left sandwiches there, but all I found was a classy pipe with a tin cover on the bowl. I sat down on a bench inside the shelter. Perceval sat down on the bench opposite, and Crowder took out his pocket-knife and began to cut his name on the wall. Perceval opened a little tin and helped himself to a Horlick's Malted Milk Tablet. I was too hungry to sit long in the shelter and walked rapidly for the next loch which lies between the mountains where they are highest. I was too hungry now to think of bathing which I had previously contemplated. Strone Scourst on the left hand side was a fine figure of a cliff-like mountain but I was too hungry to appreciate it.

I reached the main road at the head of Loch Miavaig and looked round for some houses. The largest house was off the road down by the shore and I went down a path to it to see if I could get some tea. They gave me tea and eggs and huge three-cornered scones the size of loaves. I ate several of these. It turned out to be almost five o'clock. (The path by the house was bordered with whitewashed stones. I have always liked this form of decoration which was much practised in my part of the North of Ireland). Then I took the road for Tarbert, hoping for a lift. The improbable did not occur and I walked all the way to Tarbert. This made my total for the day about twenty-seven miles and I felt properly heroic. It was not everyone, I felt, who could walk twenty-seven miles (and most of them rough going) the day after taking pills.

I had bacon and eggs and oat-cakes at about 9 p.m. in the Tarbert Hotel. These were the first oat-cakes I had eaten in Scotland. They were not home-made. I also had tea and stout—tea because the Scots don't know about coffee and stout because the doctor had said I must drink stout whenever I possibly could.

The hotel at Tarbert is the highest-grade thing I saw in this island. It has a smoke-room with leather club chairs and copies of the *Scottish Field*. On the other hand it has a very original bar—dark as bars should be (no decent bar admits the light of the sun) and traversed by horizontal bridges the width of pew-ledges on which a man when standing can comfortably rest his glass. Pew-ledges is an apt comparison for the drinkers stand silently about as if in church, their eyes reverently lowered. Once in a while they drink and then relapse into devotion.

I had a Guinness in this bar and while I was drinking it, noticed Crowder and Perceval. They were drunk.

CROWDER: Come on, Perceval old chap, give us a song.

PERCEVAL: Don't interrupt me, ducky, I'm trying to do an equation.

CROWDER: Equation?

PERCEVAL: I'm trying to prove that Flora MacDonald equals the Freudian——

CROWDER (bursting into drunken song):

Jeanie she had a loose tappet,
Jeanie she went to the Doc,
Said, 'Perhaps ye can stap it,.
I'm all run doon like a fun-fair clock.'
Doc said kindly to Jeanie
'Let's have a look at your sump'——

PERCEVAL: Don't be vulgar.

CROWDER: Doc took a spanner to Jeanie,
Said, 'The trouble with you
Is too much gin and martini
Has cracked your darn old engine in two.
Jeanie got all of a dither,
Fell into bits and died;
Doc sent the bill to her mither
And took the day off for a push-bike ride.

PERCEVAL: Poor, poor Jeanie.

CROWDER (brokenly): Yes, poor Jeanie. I never thought she'd come to it.

PERCEVAL: Never mind, ducky. Nous avons tous assez de force pour supporter les maux d'autrui.

CROWDER: Who said that?

PERCEVAL: I did.

CROWDER: Rats!

PERCEVAL: Rats? Where?

CROWDER: (singing):
Where? Where?
Under the chair
Chasing each other in the Frigidaire.

Thinking that the party was degenerating I left the bar and considered the situation of Tarbert.

Tarbert is very attractively situated on a neck of land

between two lochs—West Loch Tarbert and East Loch Tarbert. I was sorry to leave it early next morning after snatching one more stout in memory of my doctor. I left it not from inclination but because I thought that I had to go to Rodel. Someone in England had told me that Rodel was magnificent. I had got the impression that from my bedroom window I should see a fringe of foam leading to a splendid headland. The facts are otherwise and only prove once more that you should never believe what people in England tell you about other countries.

The drive from Tarbert to Rodel is very fine for the first two-thirds of the way and the driver was excellent all the way. Once you have passed the peninsula on which stands Chaipaval the road becomes squalid—littered with little tin shacks, which increase in number round Leverburgh (see page 88). I went to sleep for this part of the drive. The hotel at Rodel is at the end of everything. In front of it lies a fishing pier with a nice grass promenade leading on to it. The view seaward is blocked by an island. Everything is very quiet, not to say muggy. The hotel was having its spring cleaning. Sofas and chairs sat outside on the gravel looking as if they had no intention of ever returning to their rooms. There were a few lazy gulls. I ate bacon and eggs and also, I think blancmange.

Next morning Rodel became more alive. A boat had been out in the dawn catching herring. This was the first catch of the year. They had caught three cran. Most of them are used as bite for cod (bite seems a much better word than bait.) What I first noticed looking from my bedroom window was something large shaking itself, shaking a shining mane, loosing sequins to the sea. the net. Half a dozen men were standing on the end of the pier knocking the net against the wall of the pier so that the fish fell back into the boat. About a third of the fish fell into the water but no one minded. I admire dead fish very much. I also admire live fish, but it is more difficult to get a look at them except in places like the Fish Market at Bergen, where they swim around in tanks. When I was a little boy I used to go mackerel fishing from a motor-boat in Belfast Lough. The lines were attached to little bamboo-sticks fitted with bells and the bell rang when there was a bite. Then one hauled in wildly, the wet line leaping through one's palms and coiling round one's ankles till the fish arrived itself and bounced round the boat like a bird. I remember a shameful thrill in tearing the hook from its throat and I remember a pride in going home covered with fish-scales. The blend of smells—motor-oil and fish—was a heady one. I have never angled but I fear that I should find it dull compared with this mass-slaughter of the innocents. The sadistic urchin still persists in me and I notice him even when I eat white-bait; half the thrill of eating white-bait is that they all have eyes.

I left Rodel without having seen St. Clements, the one historical church in these islands, and took the steamer for Lochmaddy in North Uist. In the hold of the boat were two fascinating little Highland bulls, a black one without horns and a red one horned. The red was shaggy, solid, fidgeting and magnificently self-contained.

Why I went to North Uist I don't know. The hotel at Lochmaddy, being an anglers' hotel, gave me large and very classy meals but, as one of the anglers said to me, 'I can't see why anyone comes here except for fish or birds.' I did not rise for this, though I made it quite plain that I did not fish and could not distinguish between the five varieties of wild goose found in these parts. One of the anglers looked at me with some distaste and then at his companions. 'One might come here for *Art*, I suppose?' he said. 'Art?' said the companions. 'Yes, of course,' he said, 'to paint, you know. All these beautiful browns you find round here.' He then changed the subject and began to make jokes about corns.

The anglers had only caught one salmon in a fortnight, so I was very proud even to see a couple (or brace or whatever the proper title is) swim up under a bridge on which I was standing, side by side slowly against the current like horses in a state procession, magnificently stolid and solid, rather like the bulls on the boat, not to be deflected from their purpose. Swaying a little sideways like the horses in the procession or dowagers taking a doorway so as not to soil their skirts. I lolled on the bridge eating chocolate toffees and watched the little fish leaping, the small fry of the stream who had no purpose, no processional office, procreant programme, dower or bulldom. Merely episodic. Nips of light at the surface.

Near this bridge of fish they had begun to cut the peat. Peat-cutting is seasonal and the season had hardly started. I had not realised that a new cut peat was so soft—great flat cakes of gingerbread.

The bar at Lochmaddy closed at nine. A one-legged drinker found this very amusing. Frothing and gurgling through the face of an old pirate he made abstract jokes about time.

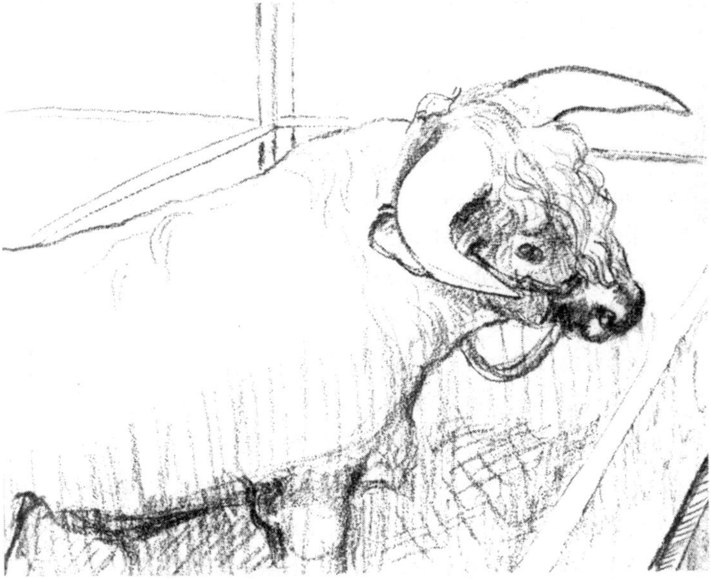

Highland Bull

The next afternoon I set out to walk across the island to the Westford Inn which lies north of Claddach. It was a desolate walk in a cold wind and rain threatening. On every side were lochs, blank and grey. As it began to rain bitingly a car caught me up and gave me a lift. It was only about four o'clock when I reached the Westford Inn, an oddly square building dumped on a desolate landscape. An ideal site for a murder story. As I had no murder to commit I felt that I had arrived too early, had no idea what to do with myself. The rain had subsided again, was now merely drizzling. I should have preferred it violent for violence of any sort was preferable to the vast unbroken dampness and dreary greydom which hung like forgotten washing from every point of the compass. I walked sadly up the road and down a lane towards the sea. But not really the sea. That which in English is called SEA, in German MEER, and in Greek *θάλασσα*, has nothing whatsoever in common with the dreary sewer that lies between Claddach and Kirkibost Island. A mere vomit of a sea, flats of slime and seaweed, a dead lagoon of limbo. The land was limbo too. Some sodden cows loitered down an aimless lane while far away in the middle of a misty tundra a man and a boy were slowly, unspeakably slowly, manuring the fields with wrack.

The next day I walked across the moors to Sollas airport. Seven miles of bog. Two men were cutting peat in a long black trench at right angles to my road. The blocks of peat were piled along the edge of the trench like sandbags. Two geese flew by silently. I arrived at the airport just as the plane landed from Skye. The air was alive with peewits, a heavy horse drew a plough to the end of the landscape and back again. The airport mechanic had a wall-eyed sheep-dog which understood only Gaelic. By now I was used to living in the sound of Gaelic and felt that the islanders were nicer when speaking Gaelic than when speaking English.

We should not, however, be sentimental about these homespun tongues. When feeling sentimental in the islands one should read Dr. Johnson who says of Gaelic that, 'It is the rude speech of a barbarous people, who had few thoughts to express, and were content, as they conceived grossly, to be grossly understood.' Dr. Johnson of course is all for the written word, does not believe in this oral culture which has made a Mecca of the Blaskets and a genius of the American negro. 'When a language begins to teem with books,' he says, 'it is tending to refinement.' Consider the Highland Bards—'That the Bards could not read more than the rest of their countrymen, it is reasonable to suppose; because, *if they had read, they could probably have written*; (italics mine: I do think Dr. Johnson's sweet, don't you, dear? Just like Aristotle.) and how high their compositions may reasonably be rated, an inquirer may best judge by considering what stores of imagery, what comprehension of knowledge, and what delicacy of elocution he has known any man attain who cannot read. The state of the Bards was yet more hopeless. He that cannot read may now converse with those that can; but the Bard was a barbarian among barbarians, who, knowing nothing himself, lived with others that knew no more.'

Note the Eighteenth Century implications:

Stores of Imagery—Chain Stores for the Educated.

Comprehension of Knowledge—an intellectual or mnemonic stomach dilated like a Rowlandson cartoon.

Delicacy of Elocution—latin polysyllables; five ways of saying the same thing.

Talking of the Eighteenth Century how Pope would have liked an aeroplane—

'The arts of building from the bee receive;
Learn of the mole to plow, the worm to weave;
Learn of the little Nautilus to sail,
Spread the thin oar and catch the driving gale.'

But he would not have said, 'learn of the peewit to fly', for the peewits compared, for efficiency, very poorly with the aeroplane—that is if the object of flying is to get anywhere. An aeroplane also does not make such whimsy noises as a peewit.

We rose up over North Uist and followed the west coast south, flying low, so that we could see the green bottom of the sea. Here and there were tiny strips of ploughland (they were ploughing everywhere in April, finishing the fields by hand where the horses are unable to turn). Benbecula was spattered with lakes, South Uist had brown mountains. We came down for a minute at Askernish in South Uist, then off again (a five minutes' flight) to Barra; I had heard so much of Barra from people in England that I feared the worst from it. One Dr. M'Pherson in 1739 wrote a Latin ode in sapphics deploring his exile as minister of God in Barra while he looked across at the 'juga ter beata' of Skye. I did not see why modern university lecturers should know more about Barra than Dr. M'Pherson. The plane dived and landed on the wet sands of North Bay at three in the afternoon. The pilot asked me if I was staying with Compton Mackenzie. I said, No, but that I would like to call on him if he was anywhere near. 'In that case', said the pilot, who had that charm which characterises all airmen, 'I will taxi you across the bay'. He taxied me over the sands and there was Mr. Mackenzie's house, the largest house not a school which I had yet seen in the islands. It was alone in the landscape. Outside it stood a dark-haired man in a sailor's jersey and with a proprietorial stare. I walked fifty yards up to him under the muzzle of his stare. 'Are you Mr. Mackenzie?' I said. 'No', he said, and then as if to explain why he was not Mr. Mackenzie, added, 'Mr. Mackenzie is in bed.'

'But go in all the same,' he said, 'Mr. Mackenzie will get up soon. He will soon be wanting his breakfast.'

Not having had any lunch and also wishing to see this ascension of a Scottish star, of the uncrowned king of the Highlands, I passed two Siamese cats and entered the house.

Dr. M'Pherson thought Barra a concentration camp, but Mr. Mackenzie prefers it to Capri. He considers it more Greek. Greek culture with furnishings from Heal's, as I thought when I entered the door.

The Scottish lions all fly off to islands—Compton to Barra, Linklater to Orkney, Christopher Grieve to the Shetlands. A hermitage on Thule—every so often you broadcast about it. Failing political balkanisation let us balkanise ourselves in our armchairs and rake in the royalties. 'Comfort', I said, walking along the passage to the drawing-room, 'where have I heard that word before?'

But Mr. Mackenzie is so much an event that I will end this chapter here and later lay down carpets for his approach. One should not bring him on too soon for there is only one of him.

VI

POTTED HISTORY

I

In the rock-pool the fingers of the anemones reach upwards and outwards, acquisitive, exhibitionist. A huge fist plunging from an unknown element causes their rapid withdrawal—blobs of jelly on the humble level of the limpets.

Similarly the city which has flaunted its efflorescence of stone, steel and concrete, frightened by a menace from the air—war, Second Coming, or the mere malaise of bigness—draws in its towers and subsides to original rock.

Lie still, they say, lie still in your corners. Show no lights by night. Curfew. A careful paucity. Forget if you can that you ever had a place in the sun.

How lucky, they say, are the people who have always been out of the way. Who have never been developed by the missionaries of wealth and culture. Whose original traits are as clear as the handwriting of a child.

The inhabitants of lands where the soil is not rich and there is no through road for imperialists or globetrotters. How lucky they say, carefully tilting the syphon, pressing the lever, how lucky are the people who have always been out of the way.

In 1919 Viscount Leverhulme purchased the Island of Lewis from Colonel Duncan Matheson. 'We will work,' he said, 'on business lines and we will have nothing to do with philanthropy. We will be able to look each other in the face, and you will be able to say to me, "we thank you for nothing but the opportunity you have given us".' A place in the sun for Lewis.

Leverhulme was not the first. Earlier was Ketil Flatnose from Norway and before him Finn with the Feinne; each man walked the dale with a brace of tall dogs on a leash. Earlier were the builders of the Callernish stones—a cumbrous but holy calendar—and the builders of the duns and brochs.

Holy men came from Ireland following Columba like the warm current of the Gulf Stream. St. Molua, a disciple of Brandan, was potent in Lewis; at his church they cured madmen with water from St. Ronan's well.

The Iberians fell before the Celts and the Celts before the Norsemen. Place-names remember the Norsemen—Habost, Shawbost and Laxay; Scandinavian faces are found in the district of Ness as they are found at Waterford in Ireland.

The Sudreys lay between the petty kingdoms of Orkney and Man, settled by truants from Norway. The Vikings raided each other, paid bloody visits in Coll, the rocky island next to Tiree of the Corn. Chieftains from the Sudreys fought at Clontarf against Brian.

Magnus Barelegs came west to reclaim the Sudreys. Fire played in the fig-trees, gushed from the houses. He went with fire over Uist, gained much gold. The islands fell under Norway.

Haco of Norway was defeated at the battle of Largs, ceded the islands to Scotland. The Gaels revived, the longships left for Reykjavik, or Trondhjem. The Norse remnant was murdered or bred out gradually. Somerled the Viking was the ancestor of the MacLeods.

Lords of the Isles, clan warfare, pillage and bloodshed. The men of the islands had little interest in the mainland and the mainland king had little check upon their doings. Donald, Lord of the Isles, intrigued with Henry of England and crossed the Minch as a rebel. At Dingwall defeated the MacKays of Caithness, fluttered the Frasers. Swooped on Aberdeen to sack it but beaten at bloody Harlaw. Alastair, his son, burned Inverness. Seventeen chieftains met at the Lord's council; none could write his own name.

Feudal government, the clansmen loyal to a despot, hereditary bards stringing traditional epithets.

MacLeod of Lewis was known for murdering his kinsmen. MacNeill of Barra from Kishimul Castle in the bay passed through the narrow sound westward to rob on the coasts of Connemara. Or eastward past the hump of Muldoanich to squabble with MacLean of Coll.

A company of crooks in Fife imagined riches in Lewis—cornlands instead of peat moors; with the backing of the greedy king they came under Lennox to Stornoway. Beleaguered by the Lewismen suffered from famine and dysentery; the remnant were dirked by Neil MacLeod amid whooping.

The Mackenzies were called from the mainland. Neil MacLeod defied them on the rock of Berisay that looks to the bevel hills of Uig. After three years was caught in a boat by treachery and promptly hanged in Edinburgh.

Lewis passed to the Mackenzies, Mackenzie of Kintail became the Earl of Seaforth. Men from Holland were brought to improve the fisheries. Hopes were all on the fish, the lands were impoverished. Here and there around a windowless Black House a couple of strips of oats twisted like emerald snakes.

Cromwell deposed Charles. Lewis looked to Holland for support against the Commonwealth, but Tromp died and Cromwell sent over a garrison to Stornoway. The Mackenzies attacked the garrison in vain and the English punished them. The MacLeods, remembering their feud, joined the English in their vengeance.

Nonconformity came upon the islands. The custom of marriage was revived. Men were baptised in flocks at the age of forty. The minister went to church between naked swords.

But pagan customs survived. Men walked out into the sea invoking the sea-god Shony offering him a cup of beer and asking him to send them sea-weed. Old women sold the winds to sailors.

Mary MacLeod the poetess was born at Rodel in Harris, became nurse to the chief's children at Dunvegan in Skye, made songs to amuse the children. For saying the wrong thing in poetry was banished by the chief to Mull, recalled for saying the right thing. Wrote a dirge for a rich man drowned who spent his wealth on music, a hunter of the wild goose, lost now in the seals' pasture. Lived to 104, taking her whiskey and snuff, carrying a silver-headed staff.

The clans quarrelled with each other, according to private feuds became Jacobite or anti-Jacobite. The Earl of Seaforth went shouting to Sherrifmuir. The 'Forty-five splashed the islands with drama. Alastair MacDonald, the Island-finnan schoolmaster, sacked by the S.P.C.K. for the making of indecent songs and after that turned Roman Catholic, joined up with Prince Charles Edward—

> O, Thearlaich mhic Sheumais,
> Mhic Sheumais, mhic Thearlaich.

He boarded a pulpit on Sunday, threw off his minister's coat and revealed the tartan.

Charles Edward lost Culloden, hid near Arnish in Lewis, thirty thousand pounds on his head. Then on an island in the long fjord of Loch Shell, then to lobster-fishing Scalpay and water-spattered Benbecula. Nine warships watched the Minch. Alastair MacDonald wrote satires on the House of Hanover, his poems were burned by the hangman at the Market Cross in Edinburgh. Charles Edward slipped into Europe, many years passed and he sank into chambering and soddishness.

Songs about him sprang into air in the glens like salmon leaping from a river—O Thearlaich mhic Sheumais. The Highlands and Islands had now a permanent focus for the age-old nostalgia of Gaeldom.

The Highland dress was forbidden and there were no more romantic causes. The islanders fought with poverty and the tacksman. Johnson and Boswell inspected the islands and watched their own phrases float like balloons to the Atlantic.

Many were evicted from their crofts, their farmland

taken for pasturage. Over in Sutherland the glens were stripped of their inhabitants. Men gave way to sheep and sheep to deer. The landlords encouraged emigration, beguiling the crofters with talk of a false Eldorado. They left their pittance on the islands to starve in Canada.

The Celtic traditions frayed in the nineteenth century. The Gordon evictions shattered South Uist and Barra. Trawlers plundered the Minch.

Calvinism cramped laughter, hell-fire silenced the fiddle. There came a blight on the potato, the plant brought to Uist by Clanranald. For a little time wealth came from whiskey.

The yellow or ruddy streams ran through the peat moors, the salmon were strictly preserved. The descendants of the chiefs became poachers. School children were slapped for speaking Gaelic.

Physical strength was still admired, and the sardonic humour of the man who, disguising himself as a corpse under a heap of wrack on the beach, kicked his avaricious brother who came to steal the dead man's boots.

The Government down in London took a few dilatory measures (Life comes into London rather than goes out of it). The fisherman-crofter was regarded as an anachronism. Up the trawler, up the marvels of commerce, the centralization of industries, the anglicization of the Gaedhealtachd.

The Great War called on the islanders. Many enlisted in the crack Highland regiments. After the War the survivors from Lewis sailed from Kyle of Lochalsh.

There were too many for the ferryboat. Three hundred went on the Admiralty boat, the *Iolaire*.

It was the last day of 1918. New year gaiety in the air aft and forward. The sea was dead calm for the crossing. In sight of Stornoway harbour the captain altered his course, took a steep angle to the right. The three hundred Lewismen knew the place like their hands, saw themselves go to their doom.

As they ran on the rock one leapt ashore with a rope, fastened the ship to a spar. At the same moment a squall broke upon the calm. The ship fell back upon the rope and listed over. The sea was all humps and chasms. Men got out on the rope, hand over hand, most were washed to their deaths. They manned the two rowboats, one was thrown on the rocks the moment it touched the surface. The men in the other would not let go of the davits, the ship keeled over further and they fell like nestlings from a nest. The men became afraid to go out on the rope to the rock. The wind increased still further. No one saw them from Stornoway. The rope snapped and the ship keeled over and sank. Only thirty odd of the Lewismen got to their homes. The island was in mourning for weeks, the shops were closed, none made jokes or love, the disaster outbalanced the War.

II

Lord Leverhulme was a grocer's son,
He learned to sell when he was young,
And all the tunes that he could play
Was 'Advertising makes it pay'——
    Over the hills and across the skies,
    By God it pays to advertise.

Bolton was his family seat
He rolled the shutters up in the street,
Said, 'It's time to be taking wing,'
So reorganised the book-keeping.

Travelled for his father far and wide
From Bolton round the Mersey-side
But small-scale business made him mope
So he patented the brand of Sunlight Soap.

He said, 'I must have a place to pitch,'
So he built Port Sunlight over a ditch,
And over in Europe he made his mark
Through the help of Monsieur Lavanchy-Clarke.*

Lever thought that life was sublime,
He went upstairs two at a time,
And the world saw Sunlight Soap expand,
To buy up Vinolia and Monkey Brand.

Lever fought elections four
But the House of Commons had a narrow door,
He saw he could try till he was dead
But he wouldn't get in for Birkenhead.

Gladstone now was Lever's pal
And he got in for Wirral as a Liberal,
And he pondered the problems by the way
Of profit sharing and the six-hour day.

Lever now made such a noise
He frightened all Lord Northcliffe's boys;

* Egyptologist and pioneer of the penny-in-the-slot machine.

They dipped their fingers deep in mess
And libelled Lever in the daily press.

Lever promptly issued a writ,
Made fifty thousand out of it;
He said, 'I've always thought it best
To work by enlightened self interest.'

He made his soap from vegetable oil
And said, 'I will grow what I have to boil,
My raw materials will be my own,'
So he bought large patches of the tropic zone.

Lever got up at half-past four,
Did his dozen on the bathroom floor,
Sent out orders during the day
To the Belgian Congo and the U.S.A.

Lever gave his hands a clap
And factory chimneys pimpled the map;
He had himself painted as the years wore on
By Sir William Orpen and Augustus John.

Lever said, 'All good business men
Should read the Book of Proverbs now and then';
He sailed the Niger black as night
And he left his name on a jungle site.

Lever smiled and stepped on the gas,
He said, 'My life will be no *impasse*,
Just you watch the speedo climb——
I'm getting somewhere all the time.'

POTTED HISTORY

Nearing seventy Lever said,
'Just one more coup before I'm dead:
I'll help those lame dogs over their stiles,
I'll stamp my name on the Western Isles.'

He bought up Lewis and then he began
To chart and build and kipper and can;
Every item was to run to scheme,
There'd be no hitches in the new régime.

He took the roof off over his bed
And he founded MacFisheries Limited
That the British householder might get
His northern herring fresh from the net.

Lever said, 'What a charming clime,'
He went up the stairs two at a time;
He said, 'It's hard but before I'm done
I'll give the Lews a place in the sun.'

But Lever's totalitarian plan
Was caviare to the Lewisman;
Our lands, they said, to us belong
And they raided the farms at Gress and Tong.

Lever said that he was afraid
The men of Lewis were retrograde,
He wrote to the Minister of Scottish Affairs
And said, 'This island needs repairs.

I'd hand them happiness on a plate
If only the fools would co-operate
But blind with Celtic mist and phlegm
They cannot see what is good for them.'

The Scottish Minister held his hand
And the raiders squatted on Lever's land,
They said, 'This Saxon Lord of the Isles
Can go somewhere else to make his piles.'

He rode round Lewis in a powerful car
And he saw that progress was anathema;
He said, 'There's nothing more I can do,
The Isle of Lewis is my Waterloo.'

He called the people together one day
And he gave them the Parish of Stornoway
And the rest of Lewis he sold in blocks
To people who wanted a shooting box.

To the Island of Harris he turned his eyes
As more adapted to enterprise;
He introduced his commercial cult——
Leverburgh is the sole result.

Leverburgh was meant to be
The hub of the fishing industry;
All that remained at Lever's death
Was a waste of money and a waste of breath.

All that remained of Lever's plans
Were some half-built piers and some empty cans,
And the islanders with no regrets
Treated each other to cigarettes.

Lever started the heavenly climb,
He went up the stairs two at a time.
St. Peter said, 'Make room, make room,
Here comes Viscount Leverhulme.'

St. Peter said, 'Don't be cross with me
But this is a mere formality;
Have you any failure to confess?'
And Lever truthfully answered, 'Yes'.

All through my life I've made my bit
From my day of birth to my obiit
And all my life I've done my best
In the cause of enlightened self-interest.

I asked for nothing but a little rope
And I paved Piccadilly with Sunlight Soap.
Organisation was my flair——
Organisation and savoir faire.

In any deed that I had to do
The thought of failure was taboo,
Only once in time till now
Did I take my hand from the racing plough.

I left my programme incomplete,
The Western Islands had me beat.'
St. Peter said, 'I'm not surprised;
To tackle Lewis was ill-advised.

The Scottish Islands are a rotten deal,
Those Celts are terribly difficile;
We find them unwilling to pull their weight
When we let them in at the Golden Gate.

They've no team spirit, they won't take part
In our study circles and community art
And at garden parties they won't concur
In speaking English—which is *de rigueur*.

No one here will consider it
The least reflection on your native wit
That the ignorant crofters, penny-wise,
Should have sabotaged your enterprise.

So welcome now to the realms divine
And sign your name on the dotted line.
You'll find the life up here a spree
For Heaven is a joint-stock company.'

Lever signed on the dotted line
And took one look at the realms divine;
He said, 'The streets are gold but why
Are there no sky-signs in the sky?'

Next day he rose at half-past four,
Pitched his desk on the golden floor.
He said, 'Where there aren't any seas
There can't be any Hebrides.'

Lever looked up from his heavenly files,
Said, 'The devil may take those Western Isles.
In Heaven now is all my hope
And I'll sell the angels Sunlight Soap.

They keep this place too blessed dark,
Send me up M. Lavanchy-Clarke;
The blest will open their blessed eyes
When they see what it means to advertise.'

He began the business then and there
And the stocks in Heaven rose like air;
The Devil's business fell as flat
As a nudist camp or an opera hat.

But far below in the Western Seas
The moors were quiet in the Hebrides,
The crofters gossiped in Gaelic speech
And the waves crept over the lonely beach.

VII

JOURNAL: BARRA

The late Stephen MacKenna went to interview Tolstoy, and was kept waiting while Tolstoy dressed up as a moujik. Some people cannot bear that kind of make-believe but I find it rather sympathetic—the luxury of the fancy collie imagining itself back in the sheepfold. The three Scottish lions whom I mentioned before, are now couchant on their islands. Being good Scots they do not suffer from self-consistency. (The Scots as a race are a Hegelian marriage of opposites—aggressive and shy, ungracious and hospitable, prudish and bawdy, sentimental and practical.) Take Christopher Grieve (Hugh M'Diarmid) of the Shetlands, who writes poems in English while swearing that no good ever came out of England and gives a salaam to Lenin while crying Ourselves Alone for Scotland. But no one can say that Hugh M'Diarmid has not got verve—

'Or a muckle bellows blawin'
Wi' the sparks a'whizzin' oot:
Or green tides sweeshin'
'Neth heich-skeich stars,
Or centuries fleein' down a water-chute.'

Or take Eric Linklater of the Orkneys, who has it both ways so successfully that he fills the shelves of Boots—a cynical guffaw in your ear and a red, red rose to your nose.

Or take the eminent philosophers, A. E. Taylor and J. A. Smith. One contrives to be an Anglo-Catholic, the other can become uncritical once a week on the Sabbath.

And now take Compton Mackenzie who lies like a barrel of gunpowder in Barra. The day that the aeroplane dropped me at his door I was not admitted to his presence. His secretary told me that she could not say when he would get up, but that when he did get up he would be busy with his mail; Mr. Mackenzie did most of his work at night; that was because it was creative; but if I left my address he would arrange that I should see him later.

I passed out again over the doormat that said Cead Mile Failte and explored the blue island which seemed to me very attractive after North Uist. I picked some primroses and spent some time stroking white bullocks. During the next two days while I waited for the royal command, I was very happy seeing Barra and generalising about the islands. Barra is a Catholic island and my lodging was full of pictures of the Virgin. There was a nice little garden, which is rare, and the cooking was comparatively good.

The islands are badly off for trees but are luxuriant with washing. Outside every house the washing hangs on line, dyke or barbed-wire fence. It hangs there through days and nights, sunshine and rain. I noticed in Barra particularly that the day is said to be 'grand' whenever it is not raining.

These islands are also notable for the number of little boys in proportion to little girls to be seen on the roads. Most of these little boys wear their hair in fringes. I had been told that the Hebrideans would mostly have black hair. This is not so. Some of them are fair but most of them, like most people anywhere in Great Britain, are mouse.

Castlebay in Barra has a large school, well windowed. When I passed it they were singing, 'Nuts in May'. The children seem a cheery lot but do not on the whole look as healthy as one would expect. (The children in the Black Houses in Lewis I thought looked pasty.)

PERCEVAL: Not perhaps that any school children look healthy anywhere.

CROWDER: Except perhaps in those up-to-date schools.

PERCEVAL: You mean those co-educational bear-gardens where no one is allowed to be repressed?

CROWDER: I suppose MacNeice went to one of those.

PERCEVAL: Certainly not; he wouldn't be so whimsy if he had. MacNeice went to one of our Grand Old Public Schools. The mild sadism of it appealed to him and he only once was genuinely shocked by its barbarity. That was a basketing.

CROWDER: A what?

PERCEVAL: In this school there was a huge barn of a building where over a hundred boys of the ages of fifteen and sixteen did their preparation and spent their spare time during the day. It smelled terribly of stables. Every

> night the boys howled for twenty minutes before the beginning of prep. You could hear them all through the school. They just howled for fun like savages working up for an orgy. One night they were satisfied. Most of these boys had to sit at their desks before prep started but a dozen or so special boys, called bloods, were allowed to run round showing off. This night the howling was worse than usual and MacNeice, astonished by its crescendo, turned in his desk at the top end of the room. He saw coming up the aisle between the desks the bloods pushing one of the huge wastepaper baskets. In the basket sat a boy who had been beaten up and had most of his clothes torn off him. His face and neck were thickly covered with red and blue paint, so that he looked liked a carnival figure until you noticed the misery of his eyes. He was also covered with ink, treacle, and powdered chalk. The bloods halloo'ed like fox-hunters and the plebs, glued to their benches, sent howl on howl to the roof forty feet above them. This was a traditional punishment applied by the boys themselves to supposed moral offenders or unpopular figures.

I had a conversation with a very hospitable schoolmistress in Castlebay who gave me tea and scones and rowanberry jelly at three in the afternoon. She spoke bitterly of the Union which she said had been 'faked up', and with romantic enthusiasm of the recent visit of the MacNeile to Barra. The MacNeiles were the old lairds who left in 1838 and were succeeded by Colonel Gordon and a period of evictions. When the present MacNeile, a handsome man with all the family traits, visited Barra from America with his bride the people of Barra greeted him like a returned Barbarossa.

'And what about Mr. Mackenzie?' I said, 'He seems to keep unusual hours.' The schoolmistress was nearly as enthusiastic about Mr. Mackenzie as she was about the MacNeile. 'In Barra, you see,' she said, 'there are so many things to distract him during the day. *The clouds and the birds.*'

In the Castlebay bar I met a handsome boatman who had a rather noble abandon of gesture and told me with devout enthusiasm of the habits of the Great (or Grey?) Atlantic Seal. Last summer he had a shot at a seal with Number One Swanshot, but this had no effect whatever on the hard skull of the beast. The curlew, he said, keep sentry for the seals in the same way as the Great Black-backed Gull keeps sentry for the cormorants. The cormorant sleeps like a fowl with his head under his wing, and you should see the islanders catching them when the Great Black-backed Gull is off duty. Cormorants are good to eat, he said, and he could never himself understand what people meant by a 'fishy' taste. He had seen the shooters in Castlebay eating gulls and what *really* beat him was why people don't eat heron which there's no young chicken to beat. [My friend, Ruthven Todd, gives me the following note on his experience with a cormorant in Mull:

'I once shot a cormorant and took it home. We roasted it, stuffed with oatmeal and potatoes which we threw away, as this stuffing is popularly supposed to draw the strong fishy taste out. Then we approached the corpse, holding our noses but we could not eat it. Next, with great courage, we hacked the flesh off the bones, curried it and put tomato sauce and pickles with it, but it was still uneatable and even the dogs would not touch it—though that may have been because of the curry. But when people tell you that cormorants are good, don't believe it.']

Barra, like South Uist, is a Catholic island. I noticed that the people were more genial than the people of Presbyterian Lewis, but far be it from me to infer anything from that. A Scottish friend of mine told me once that Scotland had found its nature in Presbyterianism. The question which then arises whether the Scots were more or less Scottish before the Reformation I leave to experts in Scotolatry. When Sunday came I was told that there was one Established Church on the island where, if I attended, a second sermon in English would be preached for my benefit after the Gaelic one. I went instead to the Roman Catholic church at Northbay which was packed. I was much taken by the mixed service in Latin and Gaelic.

Outside the church door I received my royal command to visit Mr. Mackenzie in the afternoon. I lunched on a glass of milk, which I followed at Mr. Mackenzie's with three gin-and-Its. He is one of the most autobiographic conversationalists whom I have ever met. I wholly approve of this; people who won't talk about themselves are such bores. Mr. Mackenzie cannot be called a bore.

The curse of these islands, said Mr. Mackenzie, was the dole. The dole gives you leisure. What does that mean? Leisure means living vicariously instead of working, which is living in your own right. Leisure means living like a jackal [not his phrase] on the thrills of soccer matches and the face of Miss Dietrich. But you cannot look at Miss Dietrich every day. 'At least, I can't', said Mr. Mackenzie.

He stood on a sumptuous white mat in front of his fire looking like Lionel Barrymore on the point of turning into a bird. Tiers of books rose around him to the ceiling in elegant maple (?) bookcases à la Heal. Over the billiard table hung huge paper baubles, as if in preparation for the Coronation, but study of Mr. Mackenzie's ideology suggests that they must have been in preparation for something else. His library and himself looked exceedingly comfortable. His Fair Isle pullover was almost too good a match for his green check suit. Socks of a darker green in lace-stitch pattern led the eye down to ginger-coloured monk suede shoes. Perhaps Catiline looked like this.

Yes, said Mr. Mackenzie, girls go over to Oban for domestic service merely to get their stamps. Twelve-and-six a week they get on the dole. The young people lack spirit. One could not today bring off anything like the Eoligarry raid. If only they had the spirit he would lead them forth to settle Canna, Eigg and Rhum. If only they would appreciate 'living dangerously'! It was a difficult thing to be sure of, but he tended to think that the abolition of the dole might be a salutary experiment—see what they would do when they were up against it. It was no use however arguing this point with them. MacEwen lost his seat in Lewis by denouncing the dole. Three thousand votes he lost in a block. I warned him not to, said Mr. Mackenzie.

Apart from the dole, the people of the Hebrides were demoralised by the West Wind. It was the same all down the west coast of Scotland. Whereas in the Orkneys, which are dominated by an east wind, the people were industrious and efficient.

Some years ago, he said, he could have worked a revolution in Scotland. It was not the blood that he objected to, but one could not put the clock back. The spirit of the people as a whole was dead. It might be a good idea if the Hebrides attached themselves to the Irish Free State.

Incidentally, he said, the time was ripe for a spot of trouble in Belfast. He would like, if he had the time, to go over and foment it. These things were all a matter of timing. He told me a sensational story about Carson and Greece, Lloyd George and Rumania. The Rumanian trouble cropped up first and Lloyd George cashed in on it. Otherwise Carson and himself between them—but perhaps this is confidential history, which I should not repeat. Anyway it was 'all a matter of timing'.

Wales now made as good a show as anywhere. Look at their language. And then there were those aerodrome burners serving time for their noble act of protest against a tyrannous government. They were coming out in August and he would be there to meet them.

After various reminiscences of Ramsay Macdonald, H. G. Wells ('H.G.'), De Valera ('Dev'), F. E. Smith ('F.E.'), the Queen of England and the Archbishop of Canterbury, Mr. Mackenzie told me of his earlier years. He could read at twenty months, learnt Latin at four, Greek at eight, and at eleven was translating Shakespeare into Greek iambics. It was what was called being a prodigy; one finds similar cases in music. He had an extraordinarily good memory and could run the hundred yards in ten seconds. Which is incredibly fast, he explained, thinking, no doubt, that I was ignorant in that sphere. He didn't actually run for the 'Varsity, but he played lacrosse for the 'Varsity. He jumped seventeen feet, which is now, he admitted, nothing. He had nearly been sent to Winchester, but luckily at the last moment had gone instead to St. Paul's. No great man had ever come out of Winchester. Only Sir Thomas Browne and a few bishops.

Mr. Mackenzie kept on talking. Every so often he would pop up from the sofa and stand on the white rug weighing himself on his feet and poising remarks as he poised the pipe in his hand. Behind him the fireplace was smart with green sap woodwork. Shropshire was a good county, he said, were it not for Mary Webb and Stanley Baldwin. The effect of cocoa-drinking on women was everlastingly deleterious; look at their hockey costumes. That recent best-seller, *Mathematics for the Million*, was repellent to him as an individualist. He had no use for sentimental communism.

I mentioned that I was a lecturer in Greek. Ah, said Mr. Mackenzie, now he had just finished writing a life of Pericles in 120,000 words. Of course, there was very little known about Pericles. Pericles was like Lord Curzon. He himself tended to accept much of the gossip in Athenaeus, e.g., the good stories about Sophocles. Gossip, he tended to think, would not have lasted all that time if there were nothing in it. Had I ever read the speech of Lysias for the man who caught his wife in adultery? It was an excellent speech.

Greece now—he had had the good fortune to see Greece in action; not as the tourist sees it, but signalling despatches from Marathon or hiding among Trojan irises to cut off an enemy gun. Athens he compared to New York. They had the same fine quality in the air. And the skyscrapers corresponded to the Parthenon.

The landscape from his window here, he said, was the nearest thing to Greece this end of Europe. I looked through a little ship's window inlet among his books and admired. Apart from this window the room was lit by four round windows aloft throwing light on his books. This is the room where the islanders gather on Sunday nights to play billiards.

The next three days in Barra I spent walking. In the morning I would walk from Northbay to Castlebay, hoping for a lift, and in the evening I would walk back again hoping for a lift. There are only a dozen cars on the island, so perhaps I was an optimist. On the other hand, I reckoned that as there was only one road on the island and that circular, one ought surely while walking seven or eight miles to be overtaken by one of the dozen cars. It was heart-breaking, however, to think that when one was taking the west route a car might be taking the east route or vice versa.

I got a lift one day along the east side on the back of a lorry. The lorry kept stopping to pick up people, who scrambled gaily on board and burst into floods of Gaelic. We proceeded through the island like a water-cart sprinkling laughter and Gaelic on the landscape. It was very delightful. I did not see anything notable on the east side excepting some cottages rather like the Black Houses of Lewis (but not the real thing, because they had gables) and a number of sheep, who as well as having blue dye on their rumps had their horns neatly painted an enamelled cobalt blue.

On the west side I saw a herd of seals lying on rocks in the sun. I thought they were rocks themselves till one of them turned over like a Peter Arno club-man and raised a flipper in the air. They were grey beasts and looked enormous, quite as big as sea-lions. I once dreamed that I was a seal, and there are few bodies which I should prefer for my next incarnation. It was a grand morning when I saw the seals—the Atlantic livelier than it had been, but by no means violent, moving with reserved strength like an army taking part in a tattoo. Further out were strata of vivid violets and greens and, nearer shore, the military rollers, breaking in white along the line as if suddenly saluting with white gloves.

Once more I found myself stuck in Castlebay. Each day at lunchtime I seemed to arrive at the bar and lunch off stout and chocolate. The handsome boatman had an argument with a cocky little man who looked like an Ulster garage manager. They had both been in America. The little man said that Barramen in New York had no guts, were reduced to shovelling snow. You can go

Castlebay, Barra

anywhere in the world if you've got IT, he said. (By 'it', apparently, he meant not S.A. but confidence.) The handsome boatman rolled on his tongue place-names of the movies—the Barbary Coast and 'Frisco. He told me of the cliffs on the west side of Mingulay, 900 feet up and 22 fathoms straight down; the lobster fishers let out 22 to 24 fathoms of rope.

On my last day in Barra I attempted to cash a cheque. In vain. My boat was to leave at midnight and I had fourpence with which to get to Edinburgh. I set out in the darkness and walked along the northern road to the house of Compton Mackenzie where I arrived about a quarter to ten. 'I am afraid this is the wrong time to call', I said. 'It is,' said Mr. Mackenzie, who had been summoned from his study by speaking tube. I explained that I wanted money. Mr. Mackenzie wrote a letter for me to the purser of the boat, urging him to cash me a cheque. Then he talked about the great grey seals whose habits he had observed when he was owner of the Shiants.

These Hebridean seals are exacting in their requirements. For a breeding ground they require an uninhabited island which slopes steeply to the sea on the west and gradually on the east. There must be gradations of puddles and pools for the young seals, who do not take easily to swimming. They must, he thought, have evolved late into sea-creatures.

Last night, while reviewing a novel, Mr. Mackenzie had played dab cricket. He was delighted when I told him I was very fond of the game. He explained to me his system, which allows of great variety in scoring, sides coming out for anything from five hundred to sixty. Consonants mean one; vowels mean two; three consonants running, three vowels running, a double consonant or a double vowel, mean out; a double consonant following a double consonant means that the next man is out for nought. Matches played by this system had covered his Latin schoolbooks. He searched out his Arnold's *Greek Prose* to show me his drawings of ladies in balloon sleeves. He said that his chauffeur would have driven me to the boat, but had gone to bed, having had eight teeth out today. So he gave me whiskey and parted from me warmly in the kitchen, where four Siamese cats, very large, sat on the Aga cooker.

I slept soundly on the boat, a tiny one, the *Loch Aline*—the magic having duly brought me money—and woke to see the island of Tiree, a grey, low-lying waste, and Coll, an island of rocks. Then to Oban, stricken by grey weather and early closing. I had a very bad tea in a seaside café so constructed that you could not see out of the window. The one thing that pleased me in Oban was the name MacIsaacs on a shop. I had always thought it a fiction of the music-halls. Oban has many hotels in the Scottish Baronial style. I was glad to get back to Edinburgh.

In my hotel in Edinburgh they cleaned my shoes outside my bedroom door. It was very noisy and took about a quarter of an hour. The next day I had an excellent lobster lunch at the Café Royal with Robert Dunnett of the BBC. He told me that Hector MacIver sends his lobster back to the counter if he does not think it comes from Lewis.

As I chatted to Robert I noticed two backs at the bar.

PERCEVAL: He's from the B.B.C.

CROWDER: B. be damned.

PERCEVAL: Crowder, you're drunk again.

CROWDER: Oh no, I'm not. I'll sing you a song to prove it.

Oh, the B.B.C.
 And the B.B.C.
When my cutie
 Dances alone
Her heel-taps dazzle
 On the microphone,
Oh, the BBC,

B.C.A.D.
And my X.X.X.
Was C.O.D. . . .

PERCEVAL: La plupart des jeunes gens croient être naturels, lorsqu'ils ne sont que mal polis et grossiers.

CROWDER: Rats!

PERCEVAL: Rats? What Colour this time?

CROWDER: Jade, old man, jade.

PERCEVAL: Excuse me, ducky, eau de nil.

CROWDER: Eau de nothing.

PERCEVAL: Have it your own way, ducky. I never was one to argue.

CROWDER: Eau de nothing.

PERCEVAL: Just as you say. Eau de nothing.

CROWDER (*singing*): Eau de Nothing met a nothing
Coming through the rye . . .

Robert asked for the bill, and this charming little lunch party ended.

After lunch I cashed another cheque as I had already spent the money I had got from the purser under the ægis of Mr. Mackenzie. I entered the huge bank like a temple and played the martyr to naïveté sitting under towering pillars and crunching Edinburgh rock while the acolytes all discussed whether I was to be trusted. In the end they gave me two pounds and I went to the Edinburgh Zoo to see the new tiger pits.

Then back for a period to England. I broke my journey at Birmingham, where the first thing I saw on the station was a flashy poster—Visit the Western Isles: A Wonderland of Colour. Compared with what I had seen so far, there was more colour in Birmingham. Here at last I could see that it was spring; there were leaves on all the horse chestnuts.

What else did I see in England between the First and Second Books of the Hebrides? I saw the Coronation and paddled through Regent Street that evening, a slough of sodden paper pulp. I saw Hastings, which compared very favourably with Oban. I saw a sallow alley of houses in South London with the name of Railway Grove. I saw Oxford, which I had seen too many times already—dreary Jacobean architecture, the streets obsessed by prams. I saw the Bradfield Greek play—real fire on the altar in the orchestra, but too much archæology, too many gestures by the actors, too many midges. I saw an appallingly stupid play called 'The Good Fairy', which corroborated my view that the West End stage is mad. I ran into Perceval and Crowder lunching in Rule's.

CROWDER: There's MacNeice again.

PERCEVAL: I'll have a little ris de veau, I think.

CROWDER: There's MacNeice. Don't you think we ought to observe him?

PERCEVAL: What for?

CROWDER: Mass Observation, you know.

PERCEVAL: Oh yes, Mass Observation. I think I must have a little spinach. I fancy I need some iron.

CROWDER: I'm going to have a good steak.

PERCEVAL: MacNeice, you were saying? Oh yes, I have the boy taped. Suffers sadly from fixation.

CROWDER: Fixation on what?

PERCEVAL: Oh, fixation, you know. Just fixation.

CROWDER: You think we've done him enough?

PERCEVAL: Couldn't say, my dear, couldn't say.

CROWDER: Need we go back there again?

PERCEVAL: Where?

CROWDER: The Western Isles.

PERCEVAL: Oh, the Western Isles—I'd quite forgotten about them. Yes, we may as well go back there. One place is as good as another.

CROWDER: Good for what?

PERCEVAL: Good for what, my dear! *What* an embarrassing question! Really, I should have thought by now—

CROWDER: I'm sorry, old man, I forgot. Well, here's long life and happiness.

PERCEVAL: Nonsense, my dear, who wants either of those?

CROWDER: What *do* you want, eh?

PERCEVAL: I want civilisation.

CROWDER: Oh.

PERCEVAL: And that is neither long nor happy.

CROWDER: Well, here's civilisation.

PERCEVAL: Civilisation! Requiescat in pace.

PART II

VISIT IN JULY

VIII

JOURNAL: COLL

I PACKED all my necessaries in a kit-bag bought in Spain, put over my arm an oilskin bought in Iceland and drove myself down to St. John's Wood, where I had four whiskies with my friend, Graham Shepard, in the pub at Lords. We talked about women and discussed the sad antinomy that women must be neither liars nor truthful. For while feminine hypocrisy is hypocrisy, feminine candour tends to be devastating. We then drove to Euston, where I got on the Night Scot, leaving for Glasgow at 10.45, while Graham was left with my car, to which he was welcome, as it had a punctured spare and loose tappets. I settled down in my carriage with two young men, apparently commercial travellers, and began to read *The Mind in Chains*. Shortly I went to sleep. I woke once at Crewe and went to sleep again.

I woke again—it cannot have been so much later—and saw through my window on my left (I was sitting with my back to the engine) one of the most exciting landscapes I have seen for months. To start with, it was moving, as landscapes always are from the train. Secondly, the land part of it was all in silhouette. A low bank ran along the railway line and three miraculous railings ran through the air above the bank. Miraculous because they did not seem to be supported by any uprights. (This, I discovered later by looking at them more obliquely, was an optical illusion.) The sky part of the landscape was night-blue, but like a child's painting in watercolours the paint had run out towards the bottom of the page, leaving a light band above the horizon; the rim of the land itself was purple. Straddling the lighter band was a vast star—Venus. Between the horizon and the black racing railings, or seen through the railings like a cage, was a waltz of telephone posts and pylons, the posts a heavy black, but the pylons aery and delicate. There was a surprising number of trees wandering in herds like emus. Little canals rotated and disappeared.

Then suddenly the inspired period was over. Objects were less silhouettes without yet being properly differentiated. Undynamic railings appeared with uprights. I looked at the corpsy figure lying on the seat opposite and observed a band of leg between sock and trouser. The upper sky was now a monotone of grey. Venus was higher and smaller. The pylons were no longer alive.

A town came from behind me, smoking like Gomorrah. In a huge shed without walls were fires like hungry tigers. Railway lines multiplied, divided, intersected, coalesced. Lights popped up in all directions, factory chimneys and gas-drums. The multiple chimneys of houses stuck up like inverted cow's udders. The town ran away to nothing. A single chimney on the horizon trailed a long ribbon of smoke.

Along the horizon the sky was now soft blue, purple above, then yellow, then the star. There came an oasis among hedged fields—a large factory with lights. Then many tall chimneys not smoking. Then a forest of telegraph poles and the air was full of wires—a town. A wicked little spire; more gas-drums; 3.45 on a luminous clock on a tower. Rows of houses castellated with chimneys. 'Rylands & Sons Limited' in the air on top of a factory. A signal-box full of levers. A hairy slag-heap.

Brick houses were now just recognisable as red. A long low hill lay along the eastern horizon. White mists were crawling on the fields. Poplars defied the industrialisation of England with an airy articulation of twigs and leaves. The single star which had dominated the world began to sink backwards through the sky as if into a pin-cushion. I identified a field speckled with new-mown hay. Another station came and the train came to a stop. It was Preston and 4.15.

I missed my connection in Glasgow and had to spend the day there.

I walked through Glasgow looking for somewhere to have coffee. Glasgow is as unforthputting (schoolmarm's word) in this respect as are Birmingham, Belfast, Manchester. I picked a dingy hall in green and gilt with pier-glasses, lit from above through Arctic glass. Of fourteen women in the room thirteen were dowdy. The cakes were wrapped in cellophane and the lampshades were dusty pink. Two women at last came in who had used lipstick. They had spotted veils, button earrings, fingers anxious for cigarettes. Outside I could hear the slow wash of the traffic, bobbing with litter, lost intentions, yesterday's news.

I took a tram to the Art Gallery, a huge hideous building among others, different in kind but also huge and hideous. Here are some Rembrandts, but I have a blind spot for Rembrandt. Still I liked the picture called 'The Painter's Study', and had some amusement comparing a self-portrait with Charles Laughton whom I had recently seen as Rembrandt in a film. There are many Dutch still lives with their unreal glassy precision, there are Augustus John's portrait of Yeats and Whistler's of Carlyle, there are several (alas!) Carlo Dolcis and Guido Renis, there is a Reynolds portrait of a boy in slashed mauve sleeves and with disillusioned eyes; lastly there is one of the most repellent pictures I have seen, by one Leon Felix, called 'L'Abri Enchanté'—a mauve nude with maroon flowers in her hair sits in a wood having shivers.

Downstairs if you pass through the usual Chirico nightmare of marble Fathers of the City and laocoons in plaster, you will find an entrancing room full of models of ships. These include models of eighteenth-century battleships made by French prisoners of war out of meat-bones; the rigging was originally of human hair.

I saw some maiolica and wedgwood but, thank God, no Greek vases. I have a hatred of Greek vases, (*a*) because they are ugly in shape and colour, (*b*) because they are viciously used to adorn school texts of the classics, (*c*) because the house where I have most often been embarrassed and disparaged, was full of them, whole or in fragments.

In the afternoon I went to a cinema and saw Victor McLaglen putting over heavy-weight sob-stuff well enough to rival Wallace Beery. The audience sang 'Lily of Laguna' to the Wurlitzer. I went out again and observed Glasgow, feeling like one of Mr. Charles Madge's lab boys in the world's laboratory. Glasgow contained some flags—not very many—for tomorrow's royal visit, a dentist called Calum McGaw, and a funerary window with a notice, 'Avoid waste even in your funerals'.

The 10.45 from Buchanan Street was crowded and I again took my sleep vertically. We got to Oban unpleasantly early, and I went below at once, third class, on my old friend the *Lochearn*, and slept with my head on my kit-bag which contained several books and a half-bottle of whiskey. Later I had an excellent Scotch breakfast of porridge and bacon and eggs. I went on deck while we were still passing between Mull and the mainland. The grass seemed to run down to the sea. I do not like this. There should be no philandering between sea and land. They should be puritanically separated by rocks as bedmates in fairy stories are by a naked sword.

I suddenly decided to get off the boat at Coll which is the halfway house from Oban to Barra. Coll is the island which Boswell and Johnson were driven to by a 'grandly horrible' storm and where Johnson found 'nothing much to arouse curiosity or to attract avarice'.

It was 12.0 in the morning when I walked up to the whitewashed hotel, outside whose front door are placed two vertebrae of a whale, large enough for seats. They said they were full for that night but I could sleep on the settee. Lunch would be at one. I took a stroll up the road. The place was noisy with grasshoppers and a corncrake. Buttercups, dandelions and bogcotton speckled the fields. The sun shone. This, I thought, is very much better than I expected. I went back to the hotel and ate chops.

The hotel stands below the Church of Scotland and overlooks the Bay of Arinagour, looking straight out to the very attractive Treshnish Islands which are shaped like inkstands; one of these is called the Dutchman because it resembles a Dutchman's hat. The village of Arinagour consists of a line of whitewashed houses with red corrugated iron roofs on the right-hand side of the road leading from the hotel to the pier. The pier is a sore point because MacBrayne's boats cannot come into it and much money goes in freight charges. The laird has quixotically applied to the Government for a grant, reputedly of £29,000, to make a real pier. He attributes the decay of the island mainly—so it is said—to its pierlessness. For that Coll is decaying all agree. The population has been steadily dwindling, and is now about 250, a fifth of that of its neighbour, Tiree. Half the people live on their old-age pensions and there are only about forty children. The young people are said to run off to the cities.

The guests in the hotel told me all this in the tones of complacent regret generally employed for such subjects. Yes, the inhabitants of Coll have no energy. It is the climate, no doubt. There is plenty of fish in the sea but they won't fish for it. They won't crop their farms regularly. One man's farm runs to weeds and thistles and spoils his neighbour's. No lime has been laid down on the land for forty years. There is only one farmer who makes his men get up early. In spite of all this rents are very high. Three generations ago the laird imported some Ayrshire farmers (plus Ayrshire cattle) to make cheese. A cheese factory was set up and Coll cheese became famous. But this is no more. Imported Canadian cheeses have killed the home industry.

The three other hotel guests all know the island well. One of them indeed lived in Coll but his house was at the moment let. He is a man of many activities and was just preparing to engrave a plate for a coffin. He writes out the church notices, trains the choir and goes sea-fishing in the evenings. The second guest is an angler who has been coming here for seven or eight years; he has a diffident manner and is turning bald. The third guest is a large lady with grey hair whose father was factor on a large Highland estate and who does a little weaving for a hobby, insisting on vegetable dyes. 'They ought to try to be more self-supporting,' she said. The coffin-engraver, being an old Oxonian, looked up brightly and made an epigram—'The tin-opener has killed any idea of being self-supporting.'

I had heard similar laments in Lewis. Nowhere, for example, in the islands, do the islanders make their own bread—excepting, of course, scones. All bread comes from Glasgow. And people won't bother to grow vegetables. I changed the subject and asked where I could find some seals. Over the hill by the post-office there is a bay, they said—it is only about a mile.

I walked over the hill by the post-office. The ground was very wet from last night's rain, black water shining in the hoof-marks of the cattle. Plenty of bogcotton and buttercups. The bay was full of clear green water and two or three seals' heads sticking up out of it like helmeted policemen. Sticking up very straight as if they were on point duty. The tide was out and I climbed out on the wet rocks to watch them. Two lumbered off the rocks as I approached. Around the rocks was a forest of moving sea-weed, fronded, bulbular or crinular. The grey seals swam about at a distance of twenty yards like great snub-nosed dogs. Often they would stand to attention in the water and stare at me.

After about half an hour the seals went off. I climbed some way up from the shore and slept on a ledge in the sun. I dreamed that I was playing tennis against someone whom I could not see. I then hurried back to my hotel as they eat there shortly after six. Outside the door were turkeys and cattle on the grass. Three other guests appeared whom I had not seen but who were the reason why I had to sleep on the settee. They were three brick-red and grey-haired Walking Women who had made a sensation in Tiree by bathing among basking sharks. Tomorrow they go away and I get a bedroom.

In this hotel were two books of local interest—Erskine Beveridge's archæological account of Coll and Tiree (these islands are full of duns), and a reprint of Martin Martin on the Western Isles. I am not so interested in duns but I read Martin Martin on seals—'The seal, though esteemed fit only for the vulgar, is also eaten by persons of distinction, though under a different name, to wit, ham: this I have been assured of by good hands, and thus we see that the generality of men are as much led by fancy as judgment in their palates, as well as in other things. The Popish vulgar, in the islands southward from this (North Uist), eat these seals in Lent instead of fish. This occasioned a debate between a Protestant gentleman and a Papist of my acquaintance: the former alleged that the other had transgressed the rules of his church by eating flesh in Lent: the latter answered that he did not; 'for,' says he, 'I have eat a sea-creature, which only lives and feeds upon fish.' The Protestant replied, that this creature is amphibious, lies, creeps, eats, sleeps, and so spends much of its time on land, which no fish can do and live. It hath also another faculty that no fish has, that is, it breaks wind backward so loudly that one may hear it at a great distance. But the Papist still maintained that he must believe it to be fish, till such time as the Pope and his priests decide the question.'

All the rooms in Coll Hotel are warmly lined with match-boarding—brown except in the bathroom, where it is white. The bathroom has a round window, which made me feel I was on a ship, and a hunk of Lifebuoy soap which I somehow connect with such places. After my evening meal—bacon and eggs, tea and scones—I walked out and watched a sensational sunset. The grey rocks which scatter the land went pink. The sky in the west was clear above the horizon but the clouds above it were sandwiches of peach and yellow. The clouds south-east above the blue island of Mull were gaudy with pink and amethyst. Peewits manœuvred and cried and a hen clucked quietly.

The angler gave me a whiskey; the son of the house, Hector, came in and talked of the price of petrol—including lorries, there are twenty cars on this island; my bed was extracted from the inside of the sofa. I slept, and in the morning had my best shave for months. The water in all the islands is beautifully soft. I ate my inevitable but excellent porridge and bacon and eggs, asked for sandwiches and went out walking for the day.

They had told me that the east end of the island was the most attractive, so I took the road northward from the hotel which cuts across the island (two miles in width) to Arnabost. The air was full of peewits and the fields covered with yellow flag-irises, big daisies, little daisies, buttercups and dandelions. The sheep were very white after shearing. There was a chilly breeze from the north-east but the sun shone continuously. As I crossed a rise I saw the northern sea in front of me, intensely blue across the sand-hills. At Arnabost, according to Mr. Erskine Beveridge, there is an earth-dwelling. I found its site but was unable to enter it. Whatever troll lives down there, they have closed his earth. I was disappointed as I like going under-ground.

At Arnabost one road runs east and the other west. I walked east. This island is more consistently and thickly-studded with rocks than any place I know (I am not thinking of places which are all rocks and no grass like parts of Iceland, but of places which give pasturage for sheep.) These rocks were now lilac-coloured against the dark blue sea and beyond the sea were the misty mountains of Rhum. On the left of the road, in a stretch of ground like a rabbit-warren, is one of the two burial places which are still used on Coll—some formal monuments, a white marble book with a text on it, a nicely cut slab of 1802, and many little nameless stumps of rock picked up no doubt, on the spot.

Becoming a little tired but dogged I walked with my

eyes lowered. Shadows of the peewits circled around on the tussocks. When I looked up I saw a great grey bird rise from a brook, a heron spreading its wings as an old lady don might spread the sleeves of her gown. I left the road and clambered over rocks to the beach which was covered with cattle. Towards this corner of the island there are many little sandy bays—ideal, as they say, for bathing. Flashy black and white herring gulls flew angrily crying above me, their orange beaks opening and shutting like a toy which one pulls with a string. I passed an empty schoolhouse. So far today I had met no one. Prompted to bathe by a perverse sense of duty rather than by instinct, I began to look for a place where I could get off the rocks into deep water. Coming over a rocky knoll I saw sea on my right as well as on my left—two little rocky islands, one with a lighthouse, and further to the right the familiar outline of Mull which I had seen from Arinagour. I sat down, smoked a cigarette and then slept for, I suppose, about three hours (the sun had moved well round the sky when I awoke). I woke very melancholy for I had been dreaming about running through a tunnel, the roof of which was steadily descending, worked by some sort of electricity; acetylene sparks leaped up here and there in the darkness; it had been built by the Romans but restored. Though it must be late in the afternoon I still did not want my sandwiches. The only thing to do was to bathe.

I bathed in a crescent-shaped bay whose sand was plugged with hoof-marks. The water was very cold and I did not go out of my depth. The distant sea was dark violet in colour. I ran along the sand to dry myself, realising that I had not bathed in the sea since 1929 at St. Tropez. I rejoiced in the ancient sensation of pulling a sticky sock over the instep, then ate my sandwiches and walked along the road to Sorisdale. The road ends at Sorisdale which is a picturesque hamlet on the edge of a charming bay. There are about four live cottages and four dead ones, placed at haphazard in the grass among peatstacks and poultry. The old live here and soon, no doubt, all the houses will be ruins. Weeds will grow on the thatch, then the roofs will fall in and pigeons nest in the crevices. I asked the time and was told it was a quarter to seven. As the hotel have their meal about six, I hurried the seven miles home. More buttercups, more peewits, more grasshoppers, more yellow irises, a field of green barley shimmering like shot silver. And as for rocks—the same again and again. I was home in two hours and given an excellent meal—fresh herrings split like kippers and fried in oatmeal. And scones and strong tea. A glass vase on the table contained clover. Brown lace curtains round the window framed the grey glass of the bay where the Treshnish Islands floated unwhitened by foam. The breeze seemed to have fallen.

I slept tonight not in the sitting-room but in a bedroom. Brown match-boarding reflected gleams from my candle. Outside the corn-crake went on craking indefatigably. They all think it a nuisance here, but I am sentimental about corn-crakes, remembering them from my childhood and associating them with summer.

CROWDER: He says he's sentimental about corncrakes.

PERCEVAL: I have done research on that. He lived in a house between two fields. There was one corn-crake in each. In the field to the north there was also a holy well called St. Bride's Well and a stream called the Busky Burn. To the east of the garden beyond a high hawthorn hedge was a large cemetery. The taller of the granite obelisks showed their heads above the hedge and the gardener who was apparently zany, used to level his stick at an obelisk and say, 'I'll shoot that ould fella; I'm a Frenchman.' The gardener was very rheumatic and rarely appeared before twelve in the morning. A white tom-cat which never washed, used to walk down the road to meet him and spend the day by his side. MacNeice as a little boy used to sit round with the tom-cat while the gardener would chant between strokes of the spade—

'The cat sat by the barn-door spinnin' spinnin'
By came a moose rinnin' rinnin',
"What are ye doin' the day?" quoth the cat—'

And sometimes the gardener would point his hand at the sky and talk about The Good Fellow Up There. All the time the corn-crakes to north and south riddled the garden with machine-gun fire. So now when MacNeice hears a corn-crake, an aura rises about him of childhood memories, and he expects next moment to hear the hooter of the linen mills or an outburst of orange drums.

The next day was Sunday and at twelve o'clock I went to the church (Church of Scotland) which is just above the hotel. The air outside was rich and sweet with clover. The congregation numbered under thirty. A harmonium was in the position of the altar and a bald head showed above it, like an idol, with spectacles. We sang one of the Scottish versified psalms but they cut the best verses. (The best, for a dilettante like me, are of course the quaintest.) I remembered a boy of fourteen at Marlborough, himself of Scottish descent, who versified most of the New Testament with the same appealing naïveté of inverted syntaxt—

'Command these stones to bread become.'

Afterwards, with duller intervals for prayer and lessons and a quite incoherent sermon, we sang three hymns and a metrical paraphrase from Hosea. The hymns proved once more how hymn-writing declined after the eighteenth century. The first, a distressing piece by Frederick William Faber, was followed by an excellent hymn which I did not know by one John Cennick, sung to the tune of Conquering Kings—

'We are travelling home to God
By the way the fathers trod:
They are happy now and we
Soon their happiness shall see.'

This is how hymns should be written—lucidly, simply, and with quite unpuncturable confidence. At the end of the service a lantern lecture was announced, which reminded me pleasantly of my childhood.

At lunch they told me that tomorrow there is to be a funeral. The captain of funerals is ill, so the road-mender will deputise for him. While six men carry the coffin the captain runs along the hills beside the road and shouts to his team like a rowing coach. Why they should speak of The Road-mender I do not know, as the able-bodied of the island are now all busy at road-mending. Last night some of them got drinking on the unaccustomed wages. The island is covered with barrels of tar. The surface procured is, so they told me, no use at all and wears out in a month.

After lunch I walked up to Arnabost and took the road to the left, leaving it at Grishipol (which means Pig Steading) to visit the house where Dr. Johnson stayed. This house is beautifully situated by the sea—of grey stone, with no roof, but the three broad chimneys remain. It is not a big house and is full of weeds and dung. In holes in the walls there were pigeons' nests, which contained baby pigeons covered with yellow down. If it had been Shelley who stayed here, how people would gush about this place.

I regained the road and walked on to Clabhach and Ballyhogh, passing a slated house with a black and white collie and a fuchsia hedge—the first fuchsia hedge I have seen. At Ballyhogh I tried to cut over the island to the southern road but lost my way in the huge rabbit-warren which seems to cover the centre of the island. A maze of sandy hollows and rocky knolls with rabbits of many colours sitting quizzically with their ears up. Especially black rabbits and lavender-coloured. Presumably some of their ancestors were fancies. I climbed one of the higher knolls from which I could see to the north the string of outer islands, and to the south Breacacha Castle and Mull.

Breacacha Castle, the seat of the laird, is a tall square house of grey stone and looks top-heavy in the distance, having a turret at each corner. 'Dr. Johnson,' says Boswell, 'relished it much at first, but soon remarked to me, that there was nothing becoming a Chief about it: it was a mere tradesman's box.' It was here that Boswell discovered an epitaph on a previous laird—

'Nature's minion, Virtue's wonder,
Art's corrective here lies under.'

I passed through some unaccustomed bracken and followed a little path through a meadow of purple crane's bill, so coming to a farm called Totronald and down a track leading south to its junction with the main road. Walking east again to Arinagour for most of the way I could see the sea on my right and especially the Treshnish Isles. This gave me a feeling of elation as if I wore seven-league boots. I passed another fuchsia hedge and several protected gardens. On reaching home I calculated that I had walked a good fifteen miles. The diffident sportsman was reading Anthony Trollope. 'I always like Trollope on a holiday,' he said, 'because he's not too interesting.' 'The Americans,' said the large lady, 'are buying up Hebridean wool. For their own Harris tweed, you know. As for the Japanese, they are able to put the peat smoke into theirs.'

The next day I left my most hospitable hotel and went once more on board the *Lochearn*. Going out to the *Lochearn* on the ferry-boat was an elderly man whom I took to be the laird. He wore a plaid, a kilt, a little dirk tucked in his stocking, had a grey moustache and ragged eyebrows, and complained that people wouldn't get things done. On the *Lochearn* were four tea-chests containing baby pigs from the Pig Mart at Oban. I paid for my breakfast last Friday and looked at the dreary seascape. The day was grey. The Treshnish Islands and Mull were hardly visible. In about an hour and a half we reached Tiree where I had lunch in the hotel and arranged to stay there for two nights.

The Tiree hotel is a little grander than the hotel at Coll and correspondingly less sympathetic. Tiree has many more visitors just as it has a larger population. It is said to be the most fertile of the Hebrides, is green, flat and very sandy. No rabbits are allowed on the island because if the rabbits loosened the soil, the wind would blow it away.

I was allotted a room in a tin shack separate from the hotel. The match-boarding in this room is painted a shiny cerulean. Here as I was sitting after lunch, thinking that I ought to go out but shrinking from the damp afternoon, there took place the following dialogue:

IX

DIALOGUE WITH MY GUARDIAN ANGEL

(On the island of Tiree, inside a tin shack separate from the hotel. The room is about twelve foot by eight, lined with cerulean match-boarding, and contains a bed, a chest of drawers, a washstand, two chairs, a small table.)

MYSELF (contemplatively): A room of one's own and £300 a year.

G.A.: Ahem!

ME: Who's that? You?

G.A.: Who do you think, dear boy?

ME: Well, what have you to suggest now?

G.A.: Why not go out and have a look at Tiree?

ME: Tiree!

G.A.: (unctuously): Tiree of the Corn.

ME: Well up you are in your travel-talk. I don't want to look at Tiree. Why did you let me come here in, the first place?

G.A.: Haven't you read what Miss Helen Story says? She says Tiree is a lovely land of peace and dreams and visions of eternal things.

ME: The boat does not go till Wednesday.

G.A.: There is a legend about Tiree that when the other islands sink in a general cataclysm, Tiree will keep on floating.

ME: If only it would stop raining——

G.A.: Last year Tiree had a greater amount of sunshine——

ME: Oh, do stop talking about Tiree.

G.A.: Well, what shall we talk about? Have you read that nice book by your friend Spender yet? Forward from something.

ME: *Forward from Liberalism.*

G.A.: That's it—*Forward from Liberalism.* I've always been a bit of a Liberal myself—pink as they say. And that reminds me—speaking in my professional capacity, don't you think it's almost time *you* had an attitude on these subjects?

ME: Why?

G.A.: Well, it seems to be the thing to do. Tell the world, you know.

ME: You think the world would be the least little teeny bit interested? Besides I can't tell the world what I think before I've thought it.

G.A.: Really, dear boy, you've had plenty of time to think it by now.

ME: Oh no, I've not. Anyhow I can't have an attitude. I don't even belong to the Left Book Club.

G.A.: Why don't you join, dear boy?

ME: Because I can't join a thing until I want to join it.

G.A.: Oh, yes you can.

ME: I can't.

G.A.: You mean you won't?

ME: Yes.

G.A.: Dear me. You'll never get anywhere on those principles. After all one doesn't like a thing before one's tried it.

ME: One may have an inkling one will like it. Like learning to swim.

G.A.: And haven't you got any inkling?

ME: No. No, sir, I am in a very deplorable position. My sympathies are, I suppose, Left——

G.A.: Left where?

ME: If you're going to hold me up with your Victorian habit of punning——

G.A.: I apologise.

ME: My sympathies are Left. On paper and in the soul. But not in my heart or my guts. On paper——yes.

I would vote Left any day, sign manifestos, answer questionnaires. Ditto, my soul. My soul is all for moving towards the classless society. But unlike Plato, what my soul says does not seem to go. There is a lot more to one than soul, you know.

G.A.: Undoubtedly.

ME: Look at me now, sitting in the middle of Tiree. I am in Tiree because I am writing a potboiler. Does my soul approve of that? No, sir! I am doing what I am doing, (*a*) because I need money, (*b*) because I can spare the time. But ought I to be able to spare the time?

G.A.: If you organised, you could spare still more time.

ME: God forbid!

G.A.: You feel that you are spending your time in the wrong way?

ME: Not perhaps in the wrong way, but in a negative way. Lots of people have neither the time nor the money to travel at all. Those who have both probably shouldn't have either. If, however, a man has both, he ought to travel in such a way as to improve himself and his fellows.

G.A.: Very moral you're becoming, dear boy. I'm not sure how widely you use the term 'improving'. If the concept of improvement includes amusement, it is possible that in travelling and amusing yourself you will subsequently, if you write about it, convey some harmless pleasure to your readers.

ME: Get thee behind me, Satan.

G.A.: Unless of course you maintain that there is no longer a place in the world for the frivolous pleasures?

ME: That remark which you suppose to be a *Reductio ad Absurdum*, is not impossibly the truth.

G.A.: Come, come, dear boy, you're not going to cut all the frills out of life?

ME: Frills, eh? Luxury holidays even if done on the cheap. Luxury reading and writing even in two-bob editions. Luxury thinking—popular science on the one hand, pure poetry on the other.

G.A.: Ah, poetry! You won't give that up, eh? One couldn't live a life without emotions.

ME: Who's talking of living a life without emotions? Poetry is to the emotions as my palate is to my stomach. Eating without a palate would be bad, but what about eating without a stomach? We can't consider the palate regardless of the stomach, but sometimes we have to consider the stomach regardless of the palate. In a city starving under siege we may have to ignore the palate and its long traditions of titillation.

G.A.: The poet, you mean, is a gourmet who has no place in a siege?

ME: That's what I mean. That applies at least to what is called the pure poet. Impure poetry of some sort will doubtless continue. In the same way with personal relationships. Personal relationships will continue, but we shall not always have either the time or the money for the luxury personal relationship.

G.A.: You regret that?

ME: I regret it deeply. With my heart and my guts I lament the passing of class. Of class, property and snobbery. A man for me is still largely characterised by what he buys—by his suits, his books, the meals he gives you, his chair-covers. I enjoy a book much more if I own it than if I borrow it from the library. I am both a money snob and a class snob. If I take a girl to the movies, it will add to my pleasure, (*a*) if she is rich, (*b*) if she is an Honourable. If two girls wear stockings which appear to the public eye identical and one pair cost twelve-and-eleven and the other pair cost three-and-six, other things being equal I would take the twelve-and-eleven to the movies and leave the three-and-six on the doorstep. In Hampstead I still garage my car in a public garage where I pay ten-and-six a week for it and will not take the little amount of trouble necessary to find a lock-up at half the price. It makes me feel grand to have credit at my garage and when I fill up with petrol, merely to sign a docket for it. I like to be able to say *my* garage, *my* car, *my* overdraft.

G.A.: If you'll excuse me, dear boy, I think that all that is adolescence.

ME: In September I shall be thirty. How much longer do you think I shall take over adolescing?

G.A.: Not being a psycho-analyst I could not say. But let us look into this question. The case against you is black. On your own admission you are preoccupied with luxury values—diseases like the pearl in the oyster. But are these your sole occupation?

ME: I cannot say but it seems to me so likely that they are that I should be ashamed to join any crusade for the betterment of the world, knowing as I do that my motives would again be snobbish, even if the snobbery is inverted.

G.A.: But, my dear boy, there must be lots of snobs even in the Communist Party.

ME: Doubtless there are, but do they do the party any good?

G.A.: I don't see why not. A few bad motives to an action won't invalidate the action.

ME: A *few* bad motives perhaps not.

G.A.: Now that is just what I am getting at. We want to sort out your motives, reactions, values. Do they all without exception presuppose a world of snobbery? When you take your girl to the movies, are you merely taking her stockings and her title?

ME: Supposing she has either.

G.A.: Supposing she has either, ha, ha. You see what I mean though? Are you chiefly interested in the girl or in the accessories of the girl?

ME: You expect me to say in the girl?

G.A.: Of course I do.

ME: Of course nothing! I think it very possible that I am chiefly interested in the accessories.

G.A.: Really, dear boy—

ME: For the sake of hypothesis suppose we subtract her accessories. Suppose we subtract her stockings, shoes, make-up and permanent wave. There remains her body entirely ungarnished and there remain certain mannerisms, most of which will fail to work without the garnishments. In any case all these mannerisms themselves—gestures of the hand, poise of the foot, intonations of the voice or eyebrows—must also be dismissed as accessories, imitated from snobs by a snob and practised for the seduction of snobs. Cut all these out and you are left with mere body.

G.A.: What about her mind?

ME: Oh, her *mind*! We must do the same with her mind. Cut out all the tricksy ideas, the pseudo-sympathies, the pseudo-insights. What remains?

G.A.: God knows.

ME: There remains mere mind and mere body. Mere body might do for D. H. Lawrence but mere mind seems to me entirely dull. A mind must be conditioned by education and social context. Now all the people I know have been conditioned by snobbery—

G.A.: But not entirely by snobbery.

ME: There you go again with your not entirelys. All the people I know have been conditioned either entirely by snobbery or so damn nearly entirely that any idea found in them which has failed to be so conditioned, is either the minimal residue of their dull animal nature or a scrap of abstract thinking (2 + 2 = 4) which through mere inertia has failed to attach itself to the practically all-embracing snob Weltanschauung of its owner.

G.A.: Bless me, dear boy, you are talking like an absolute cynic.

ME: You think so?

G.A.: You used the phrase 'dull animal nature'. Leaving out the 'dull', which seems an unnecessary epithet, are you not perhaps underestimating the influence—often for good—of that side of the human being? Our brother the ass cannot be described as a snob——

ME: No, but he can be harnessed to the snob-cart. Lawrence was a snob undoubtedly.

G.A.: Because he deliberately cultivated what ought to be spontaneous. But when a man is a perfectly straightforward animal——

ME: He just has a damn awful time of it seeing that the world is what it is. Anyway what is that to me? You can't expect me to be a perfectly straightforward animal. I belong irrevocably to the lost intelligentsia.

G.A.: Let us try the other tack. Let us admit that in your case it is useless to ask you to follow your instincts, to re-become your ancestor the Irish peasant——

ME: There was nothing straightforward about him. Religious superstition, puritan taboos——

G.A.: Yes, yes, but we are leaving that now. We are leaving escape by the body and thinking of escape by the mind. You say that everyone's mind—at least in the case of intellectuals—is inevitably conditioned by snobbery?

ME: Yes.

G.A.: Then where does the pure scientist come in?

ME: Where does *who* come in?

G.A.: The pure scientist.

ME: He doesn't. He can't come in because he hasn't got any legs. Not if he's really pure, he hasn't.

G.A.: How you quibble, dear boy. When I say pure scientist I am not thinking of an individual man but of an individual *qua* scientist, in abstraction from his other qualities. Surely most of us at times are able to suppress the other side of ourselves—the personal, sensual or acquisitive side of ourselves—and consider the world or part of it purely objectively—as pure objective pattern which we get to know and then contemplate purely for the pleasures of knowledge and contemplation.

ME: Largely for the pleasure of showing off our knowledge in the drawing-room. Have you ever heard Aldous Huxley take part in a conversation?

G.A.: Again, dear boy, you are confusing things. I do not say that when one acquires knowledge, one is not extremely pleased to show it off. But I do believe that in the acquisition and exercise of knowledge the main factor is a disinterested desire on the part of the Ego to come into intimate contact with the other, the objective world.

ME: You think so? You are helpfully suggesting in fact that during the Untergang, the collapse of civilisation, the noblest function of a person endowed with a brain is to sit on the ground and count the legs on a centipede. The waves of war flow forward——

G.A.: Well, you can't be like King Canute and tell the waves to go back.

ME: No, but one might be like Noah and set about building a boat.

G.A.: Why don't you, dear boy, why don't you?

ME: Others will build boats but not me.

G.A.: Why not you?

ME: Because I have no experience of manual labour.

G.A.: You say that a little too smugly. Dear boy, my suspicions are aroused. You speak, on your own profession, as one of the lost. Speaking as one of the lost you ought either to be tearing your hair or going to perdition like a Stoic. Giving you the once-over I observe that your face is too fretful for a Stoic and that your hair does not seem to be torn. You sit there and say, 'Others will build boats but not me. I should be no use at building boats. I should only get in the way.' You seem to forget that it is never too late to learn, that the hands can learn new trades——

ME: Like Tolstoy, I suppose, dressing himself up as a

moujik. Recipe: cowdung on the boots and a face wincing from excess of humanity.

G.A.: You are just being perverse. You are saying, 'If I walk from London to Reading, it will look as if I am a hiker. I am no hiker, so it would be just a fake. I should walk there on false pretences. Therefore I will not walk there. Therefore I cannot walk there. Therefore I am lost because London is a doomed city. *Quod erat*, you say, demonstrandum and give me a brandy.

ME: So what?

G.A.: Well, you damn little fool—dear boy, I mean—suppose you set out and walked from London to Reading? Suppose you got to Reading, you'd be in Reading, wouldn't you? Whether you were a hiker or not a hiker, or thought you were pretending to be a hiker or thought that other people would think you were pretending to be a hiker, anything you happened to think about your own thoughts on the subject of walking from London to Reading, could not possibly undo the fact that you had got to Reading. And don't you go telling me that Reading is a relative entity and that Reading for you is something different from Reading for John Brown.

ME: Well, it *is* something different.

G.A.: Oh, forget you've been at Oxford. Reading's a place where they make biscuits. A whole library of nineteenth-century subjective idealism won't alter the fact that Reading's a place where they make biscuits——

ME: But what is important——

G.A.: What is important, you will say, is not the biscuit factory but your—Louis MacNeice's—emotional reaction to the biscuit factory or your—Louis MacNeice's-astigmatic and purblind intellectual concept of what a biscuit factory is, might have been, ought to be or can't be. That's what you're going to say, you little squirt. Well, if you want to say that, if you want to be damned not for a positive sin but for the mere colourless inertia of a person who won't soil his individuality with action—You know what you're like? You're like a snowman waiting for the thaw.

ME: There's nothing else a snowman can do.

G.A.: Perhaps not, but supposing the snowman is a human being dressed up as a snowman? Who did it for a rag or because he was temporarily mad. Well, when the party is over or the madness subsides, is that man to go on standing out there as a snowman, making it a point of honour never to stop pretending? Forty years on, getting colder and colder——

ME: If it's getting colder and colder, there won't be any thaw.

G.A.: Bah! When you are beaten to the draw, you always go off into frivolity. Are you or are you not going to give up being a snowman?

ME: Mais où sont les neiges d'antan?

G.A.: Are you going to, partly out of pique, partly out of vanity, but mainly because you are just darn bone lazy, wilfully espouse a life of outmoded triviality and inaction——

ME: Eloquent you're becoming in your old age!

G.A.: I've had to speak on similar lines before. To the runts of classic aristocracy playing at cottabos, to the powdered self-deceiver tapping his snuff-box, to the armchair speculator, the saint in the private rockery. To all who would sell their birthright for forty winks, saying, 'Apres moi le déluge'. Going down most of them not in a glorious cataclysm, not in a noble twilight of diehard gods, but bogged in the quicksands of their own superannuation. Well?

ME: Well what?

G.A.: What course are you going to take?

ME: Is it a hammer and sickle I see before me?

G.A.: Yes, dear boy.

ME: (singing):

He took up the hammer
And hammered the wheat,
He took up the sickle
And cut off his feet.

G.A.: Shut up.

ME:
He took up the hammer
To open an egg,
The hammer fell down
And it fractured his leg.

G.A.: Shut up.

ME:
He took up the sickle
To tickle his wife,
He cut her in pieces
And ruined her life.

G.A.: Very, very funny, dear boy.

ME: (gratified): You think so?

G.A.: No, I don't think so. (Takes up his hat.) Good-bye.

ME: Where are you going.

G.A.: I'm going to the root of the matter.

ME: What matter?

G.A.: Ha, ha, dear boy, wouldn't you like to know?

ME: I'll come with you.

G.A.: You can't.

ME: Why?

G.A.: Because you're on an island. The boat doesn't leave till Wednesday.

ME: Then how are *you* going?

G.A. (showing his wings): You forget I have these, dear boy.

ME: Oh those! I didn't know they worked.

G.A.: They didn't. I've had 'em repaired.

ME: I never had any anyway.

G.A.: So you say.

ME: *I* never had any wings.

G.A.: So you say.

ME: What do you mean, 'So you say'?

G.A.: I mean, 'So you say'.

ME: Oh, go to hell.

G.A.: I'm going, dear boy, but not to hell. I wouldn't need wings for that. Good-bye, dear boy. Bless yourself and keep yourself. If I haven't the time to look in on you again, I'll send you a packet of forget-me-not seed. Il faut cultiver votre jardin.

(He goes out and shuts the door gently. Rain falls on

Tiree. Westward the leaden Atlantic stretches towards America; the shade of Columbus argues with the mutineers. I look out of the window and see a Viking longship run up into the harbour. Twenty Norsemen with horned helmets come striding up towards my shack. They say with one voice—

We are coming to get you,
We are coming to get you,
You thought you were safe in your corner,
You thought you were safe on your island;
The boat will not go till Wednesday,
There's no escape from the island.
If you had wings you could fly but you have no
wings.

I stand in the window unable to turn away. The horned heads move up huge as Molochs. Behind their spears the rain falls on the barren flagstaff and the first tee of the golf-course.)

X

JOURNAL: TIREE, BARRA AND VATERSAY

I WAS in Tiree from Monday to Wednesday and it rained almost continuously. Last year it is said that Tiree had the record amount of sunshine for the British Isles. This may be so but in my opinion Tiree is a wet place, almost submerged by the sea around it and soused from the rain above. In winter the boats often refuse to call here and visitors may be imprisoned on the island for a week or ten days. There is a legend that when the other islands, even those with mountains, sink in some cyclic cataclysm, flat Tiree will still keep her head above water. A depressing thought. Unlike most visitors I very much preferred Coll. Tiree has macadam roads and a meteorological station—the local schoolmaster rings up (or wires?) the Air Ministry three times a day. Tiree also shows her civilisation by having no licence—the traditional policy of the dukes of Argyll. And she has a number of rather primitive golf-courses, most of the holes, as a visitor remarked to me, being controlled niblick shots. Instead of flags the greens are marked by canisters or bottles upon sticks.

I saw a concrete house being built—if building is not too good a word for this indefinite and sloppy-looking process. A framework of planks is erected into which are poured cement and stones from the beach. It must be fun, of course, when you remove the wooden mould, and, lo and behold, there is the house of your dreams. I met two young men, visitors, unshaven raw-boned Scots, walking on the beach in shorts, collecting for mementoes the handsome glass balls which are used as floats for nets.

There is no peat on Tiree but the hotel gave us a coal fire each evening. The guests, all Scottish, sat round and discussed the world. There was a business Scot who often did business in Ireland and, not knowing my nationality, said all the usual (and indisputably true) things about the Irish. He was particularly scathing about De Valera's sham industries—putting liver salts into tins, cutting boot-laces into lengths. His daughter, a plump schoolgirl, was enjoying the island thoroughly, bathing and fishing. She had a tin of her own at meals containing lemonade powder, called Creamola Foam. Her mother, similarly plump and equally genial, said at some length that Bridge was a great test of character. A tall young man with prominent ears, hiking the Highlands with his wife, talked to me about abstract photography; the wife thought that this was a perversion. A piano-tuner with the gross grace of many commercial travellers, short in heavy plus-fours, black hair brushed from the forehead and looking like a rather wicked ram, told how he was the only person who had ever taken a motor-bike to Iona. It upset the dogs and enraged the inhabitants, and he could never get beyond second gear. But most important was the young man who told fortunes.

He had a toothbrush moustache, fine brown eyes and a very loud sports coat. He swept the cards in a semicircle on the table and said, 'Pick nine from the left'. A quaver at once came into the visitors' voices. I have never seen an amateur tell fortunes so convincingly. He was all the more convincing in that many of his prophecies were unpleasant—illnesses and deaths. He told us that he had given it up for a bit after he had told someone that within a week one of his relations would be brought home on a stretcher after a motor accident and another would fall downstairs; both which things happened. I asked him to tell my fortune. He swept out the cards and said, 'Pick nine in this order without going back on yourself'. 'Everyone is picking this tonight,' he said showing me the Ace of Spades. Then he studied the nine cards. 'There is a fair girl, or maybe mousy brown, very much in love with you,' he said. 'Oh', I said. 'I'm afraid I can't tell you these cards,' he said, 'you are too near to me altogether. I can see all your thoughts.' 'Why?' I said, 'are they bad?' 'No, they're very good,' he said, 'but I really couldn't tell you these cards.' He was genuinely embarrassed. So we went on to the next stage and had some sticky going over a big contract which was coming to me. Then he laid nine cards down in a certain order on the table—'That is your head and that is your feet, etc.' A tenth card was laid over my head, the something of spades. 'Are you studying something?' he said. 'That is the study card.' 'No.' 'Well, by studying I mean are you taking notes about anything?' 'Maybe,' I said, anxious not to be discovered as a writer. 'Cut the pack in three like this,' he said, 'this is for your wish. And keep wishing all the time you do it.' He swished the three piles along the table and said, 'Pick a card from each.' There came out the Queen of Clubs with spades on either side of her. 'No,' he said, 'you won't get that wish.' For one who is a scoffer, I was unreasonably depressed by this experience.

On Tuesday evening a gale got up. I was reading the Spanish poet Lorca's *Lament for a Bull-fighter*—Ay qué terribles cinco de la tarde!—when a boy came running to the hotel to say that there had been an accident at the pier. Someone had been hurt in a yacht which had run over from Iona. They were bringing him up to the hotel. I always think that a most alarming phrase—'they are bringing him', it implies such log-like helplessness. We heard a car on the gravel but no news. The piano-tuner made jokes about the 'corp'. I went on reading Lorca—an unremitting barrage of physical sorrow, the terrific contrasts of Spanish shadow and sun.

Gaelic poetry is full of the terror of storms. There is a thrilling long poem by Alexander Macdonald ('The Manning of the Birlinn') in which he piles wave upon wave of hyperbole or, as Corinna would have said, sows with the whole sack—

Till the sea, like a great mess of pottage,
  Troubled, muddy grew
With the blood of many mangled creatures,
  Dirty red in hue—
When the horn'd and clawy wild beasts,
  Short-footed, splay,
With great wailing gumless mouths
  Huge and wide open lay.

The visitors went to bed except the businessman, the piano-tuner and myself. The piano-tuner told a story about a parson with false teeth. Then the business man went to bed. The piano-tuner and I were sleeping in two of three rooms in the tin annex. We were told that 'the accident' had been put in the third, so were not very anxious to go over. 'It's a pity this island is dry,' said the piano-tuner. I told him I had a little Irish whiskey and went over to the tin hut to fetch it. There I found a young man in shorts and a sweater on guard at the door of the third room. 'There is a patient in there,' he said, 'the doctor is with him now.' I learned what had happened. The man had been trying to fasten up with a rope when his foot slipped on the diving yacht and he caught his head on the pier. He had put his teeth through his tongue; the doctor had just been putting stitches in it. He would be all right.

The next morning was wet again. I read a pamphlet written in 1883 by the seventh Duke of Argyll—an eloquent defence of his management of estates in Mull and Tiree. He denied evictions and maltreatment of widows, defended the policy of emigration to Canada, deplored the over-population of Tiree, vigorously opposed the subdivision of crofts and contemptuously depreciated common grazings—'even when peace is kept and quarrelling avoided, it is done only by the sacrifice of that spirit of individuality in enterprise and improvement which is the life and soul of all industrial pursuits.' I admired the Duke's gift of protestation but am in no position to decide whether he did not protest too much. One of the complaints against him, seconded by a Professor Mackinnon, was that he exacted rent from the kelp-burners who dried their kelp on the same land for which he exacted rent from crofters. To this the Duke plausibly replies—'If Professor Mackinnon were to give two distinct courses of lectures, one on the Celtic language, and another on the Sanskrit language, and if he were to charge, as he would have the best right to do, two separate fees for these, then two separate rents would be raised from the one piece of brain belonging to Professor Mackinnon.'

The population of Tiree is now about 1250. In 1846, the year of the potato famine, it had reached the peak figure of 5000. Undoubtedly five thousand is too many for such an island, but it seems regrettable that here, as in the other islands excepting Lewis, the population should still be dwindling steadily. The islands perhaps can only be saved if they are turned into rest-cure stations for people from the world of success, but it is doubtful if this will save the islanders. The hotel-keepers, green-keepers, bankers and bartenders will almost certainly be imported with the visitors whom they are to tend. The natives have not got the money-making conscience. As it is, they do not even hire out boats for pleasure.

The *Lochearn* was two hours late coming from Coll and I was able to have lunch in the hotel. The piano-tuner played 'Daisy, Daisy' on the piano. The rain fell on the green flats of Tiree. Little was visible. I was glad to get on the *Lochearn* and sail for Barra. Twenty-eight motor vehicles saw us off at the quay. The journey took about five hours. The piano-tuner, who was also going to Barra, asked me to 'come and have a wet', but all the stewards were in bed. 'Having forty winks' as the piano-tuner put it. Most of the passengers were sick. I travelled first and paid five shillings for a third.

When I went out on deck we were sailing straight for Muldoanich, standing up abrupt, a mottle of grass and rock. To its right lay Barra, and to its left the string of hilly islands to the south. I had a resurgence of boyish enthusiasm—*veteris vestigia flammae.* This is how Hebrides should be—a string of misty hills surrounded by water. Mist sat on the top of Muldoanich which is only five hundred feet. The rain stopped and there was comparatively a gaiety in the scene when we entered the sound between Vatersay and Barra, having passed a few drifters outside. Light broke through the clouds in the west over the narrower channel, which is guarded by the island rock on which is the guiding light; the light at this hour was not lit.

I decided to stay in the hotel where once more I was assigned a room in an annex of corrugated iron, reached by walking over a small plot of grass where a baby bullock was tethered. I had some herring for my tea and once more regarded Barra. Castlebay harbour looked better than I remembered it perhaps because of the seven or eight drifters which lay there at anchor. In the bar were a few taciturn fishermen. This is being a very bad season at Castlebay. Catches are averaging three cran (a cran fetches £4 10*s.* 0*d.*) In good years there have been 150 boats in the bay, 200 cran in a boat.

It gets dark late in the islands—a good half-hour later than in London—but before dark the drifters lit up and the bay was dotted with lights. A party of Edinburgh

University students who have been camping at Northbay for a fortnight, came down to wait for the *Lochearn*. (The *Lochearn* after reaching Castlebay goes up to Lochboisdale, then back to Castlebay some five hours later on her return journey south.) These students have been making 'a biological survey of the island'. I asked them what that meant and they looked surprised and began defining biology. They have done insects, birds, flowers and creatures in the sea. They had brought their own food with them from Glasgow. Men and girls, they wore shorts, slacks or kilts. They had to wait till 2.30 in the morning for their boat.

Crowder and Perceval looked at them with distaste—

CROWDER: I can't bear students.

PERCEVAL: I can't bear students if they're women.

CROWDER: I can't bear women if they're students. They're all so awfully mental.

PERCEVAL: I have never met a woman who was not mental.

CROWDER: Oh, look here, old man——

PERCEVAL: I admit that there are certain women who are also physical.

CROWDER: Thank God there are!

PERCEVAL: *You* thank him, ducky.

In the morning I had breakfast reasonably late and then looked out at the bay. Something had gone wrong with it. The something was gulls. Over all the little piers of the herring industry gulls were swooping and banking—so many of them that you seemed to see the scene through a shaking curtain of white beads. It was like news-films of celebrations in New York when the skyscrapers snow down bits of paper. Or like a slide under the microscope—circulation of graceful bacteria. I walked down on to the piers. On each pier four or five women—burly in gum-boots and flowered aprons, with handkerchiefs tied round their heads—stood behind a huge wooden trough. The right hand gutted the herring and flicked the guts into a small wooden bucket on the trough; the left hand with the movement of a swimmer flicked the herring backwards into a bucket on the ground. They worked very fast. A couple of women in the background stood beside barrels of salt and salted the herring. The gulls that were not in circulation perched on the roofs of the fish sheds or whitened the hill behind the town. In one of the sheds was an excellent picture in tar—a fisherman in a sou' wester and with a pipe in his mouth holding out his hand to a very Moulin Rouge young lady with a fur round her neck; the medium of tar gave a Toulouse-Lautrec effect to the eyes.

After eleven I went up to the bar. Three men leaned against the bar and their three cigarettes, strictly parallel pointed across it like ships' guns. They ordered beers and whiskies simultaneously and sipped them alternately. A middle-aged man in abstraction stared at the romantic landscape which advertises John Begg's Whiskey.

If I had dinner in the hotel, it would cost me three-and-six—I preferred to take beer and a bar of chocolate and then go walking. I walked west past the fish-piers and shacks, untidily bordering the bay, lines of washing blown out like carcases of pigs, and went up over the shoulder of Ben Tangaval to get a view of the narrow part of Vatersay Sound. The ground was marshy, lathered with bog-cotton, but when I got over the top I had rocks to walk on and clambered westward above the Sound. The sun had come out by now and Vatersay Sound was blue and pimpled with sunshine. Over in Vatersay three men walked as in a dream through a yellow field. Vatersay was dream territory because unattainable. It has an attractive coast with stretches of white sand.

One of the dream figures put out in a rowing boat and rowed over the Sound. He signalled to me and asked did I want to go over. I ran down the cliff *ripae ulterioris amore* and jumped into his boat. He said that he had thought I was George Smith. The water was beautifully green above a sandy bottom. I disembarked, thanked my very amiable boatman (who had forgiven me for not being George Smith) and began to walk round the island anti-clockwise. I walked through fields of silky barley and clover, meadowsweet, ragged robin and poppies. Cutting across the western corner I reached a little bay looking south-west over the Atlantic. I picked up a rounded piece of wood polished by the sea to the lustre and lights of moleskin. The sand shelved very steeply and was flanked on each side by rocks. I sat on the rocks, sloping like the roof of a house, and watched the sea.

Perceval and Crowder sat on the rocks also, Perceval spreading out his ordnance map to sit on as he is afraid of rheumatism.

PERCEVAL: The waves' cavalry advances deliberately, momentously——

CROWDER: Looks jolly cold, eh?

PERCEVAL: The waves' cavalry advances deliberately,

momentously—and the explosive filigree of foam fills the air and vanishes—appears, disappears, reappears in a moving dialectic of instantaneous pattern. Even C. B. Cochran in his most imaginative moments could not present such a lavish and intricate spectacle——

CROWDER: No, but there'd be more girls about.

PERCEVAL: Girls! Didn't I tell you you don't appreciate nature! The waves' cavalry—

CROWDER: The waves' cavalry advances-dress by the right. Full marching kit will be worn, kilts and sporrans of seaweed. The regimental porpoise will take his usual place between the first and second platoons of Company C——

'This is the way the mermen ride—
Slippety slop, slippety slop . . . '

PERCEVAL: Shut up, my dear. I can't bear people who're whimsy.

I agreed with Perceval and moved some yards to the left.

The rocks on which I sat had patches of gnarled red and streaks of alabaster. As I watched, the horizon turned indigo, promising heavy rain. But the rain that came was slight and soon over and the horizon recovered its blue. I walked round the shoulder of a six hundred-foot hill and suddenly got a view of the islands—the series including Pabbay and Mingulay. I have a feeling that I shall now never walk on Mingulay. I picture it as a sort of St. Brandan's island inhabited by happy seals and innumerable birds; on the eastern side is a village of ruined houses where the Red Scholar was born; silence lies coiled around it like contour lines in a map—you climb from silence to silence till you lie on the peak of the island and look to the west which is nothing—'nothing, of nothing; cease your idle questions.'

There were many blue butterflies and others with crimson spots on green. I followed the rocky coast, clambering above it on the hillside, till I came to a long bay of white sand beyond which were houses. At this point the island narrows to a neck—a sandy waste of ragweed. Opposite my bay on the west is Vatersay Bay on the east. Having passed a nine-foot granite obelisk with an illegible inscription, evidently a War Memorial, I met an old man and said, 'Good morning. What is the time?' He said, 'Good morning. The time is just turned four.' I cut across a series of mounds and sandy hollows—the sort of place that they call a natural golf-course—to a little bay on the south. The sand here sloped very gradually and was beautifully smooth and firm. I lay on it and wondered whether I should bathe. Before me lay the Island of Sandray, the other islands rising in terraces beyond it. I closed my eyes and listened to the sea, no longer voluble but maundering with lazy sibilance, the dying falls of involved and senseless sentences. The sun shone but it was not hot. I decided not to bathe. With some difficulty I cut back to the northern side and made a detour round two more sandy bays. There are very few shells on these strands though the sand itself seems to be compounded of shell. Overlooking the sea was a tiny house, shapeless as if built by some animal, the thatch tied down with ropes. I saw a little motor-boat just putting off from some rocks and ran down in time to get a lift to Castlebay. Shadows of white clouds floated on the hills of Barra and a white husk of a moon had appeared out of nothing over Vatersay. It was about six o'clock. In shallow water near the island with the guiding light the propeller caught in long weeds and the engine stopped. 'This is a fine place for young skate,' said the boatman complacently and waited till we had drifted out of the weeds and the engine could start again. In the bay lay a smart white steam-yacht and we changed our course to look at it. The upper deck was covered with an awning not very appropriate to the latitude. When I reached the hotel the others were eating tea. The others were the piano-tuner, two commercials and two middle-aged ladies. The latter had been picking wild flowers. They were very excited by the bay on the west coast which the brown stream runs into; in the sun the whole bay had been amber. I stuffed myself with herring while they all made jokes about a fly which was sitting on the cakes.

After tea I strolled down to the pier. Three of the people on the steam-yacht had just put off for the yacht in a very grand motor-boat. A stocky little pot-bellied blue serge hard-bitten man in a light cloth cap was eloquent over his grievances. 'Them on their cushions!' he said. 'Just now I saw a rowing boat come over from Vatersay and a woman was pulling the oar. I only get three pounds fifteen a week but I do more for my fellow-creatures than the likes of them in that yacht ever did.' He was a

Glasgow engineer, fifty-three years old, having a holiday in Barra after a nervous breakdown.

Today's *Daily Record* had just reached Barra by 'plane with the news of the fines imposed on the Barra motorists who had refused to make their licence payments. These fines amounted to £112 13*s*. 0*d*., while expenses came to £30 3*s*. 6*d*. In the words of the *Daily Record* Sheriff Inglis achieved a high standard of judicial crispness in dealing with this motorist rebellion . . . 'I regard this case,' he said, 'as peculiarly unfortunate and a grievously ill-chosen example of endeavour to show parochial independence of national obligations.'

Mr. Maclachlan, the Procurator-Fiscal at Lochmaddy, in pleading for the Barra motorists maintained that 'they were a loyal community and nothing had shown that more than their service in the War. Highlanders and Islanders were continually to the fore.

THE SHERIFF: How many Highlanders and Islanders are there in these names before me?

Dr. Bartlett didn't sound like a Highlander. Mr. Compton Mackenzie was certainly an Islander in the sense that he almost invariably resided upon an island, but Barra was only the most recent of many. Smith and Haggarty did not suggest Highlanders to him.

The Glasgow engineer was highly indignant at this defeat of the Barramen. 'If they weren't all damn cowards,' he said, 'they'd choose to go to prison. They'd be out in a week. There's nothing in this world ever been got without agitation.' The people in Barra were no good, he said. Ninety per cent of them wouldn't work if you offered it them. His wife's mother, a poor old woman who lived in Barra, wanted stones collected for a new house and could hardly get men to do it for ten shillings a day—ten shillings a day, my God! He switched over to Hell. 'There's no such damn place,' he said; 'God couldn't make a place more fiendish than this present world. I believe in God,' he said, 'but I don't believe in Hell. No matter what anyone says.'

I met the piano-tuner and we had a drink in one of the three little rooms at the back of the bar. I had not seen these very unusual rooms before. You get your drinks through a pigeon-hole opening on the back of the bar. The room is about seven-foot square, lit from a skylight at the top of a seven-foot well. Dark consequently, and like a cell in a gaol. One little table covered with rings of liquor. 'Here's mud in your eye,' said the piano-tuner. He suggested that we should walk over the hill east of the bay and have a look at the evening.

This we did, passing a couple of deserted Black Houses. Over the brow we got a fine view of Muldoanich but nothing else was visible on the sea. We turned home again and saw the sun shining on Kishmul Castle—'A good sun effect,' said the piano-tuner. And as we got back into the town, 'The scenery must have been pretty good here today,' he said, 'judging by that washing-line,' he added. I looked up and saw a washing-line with some towels and two girls' bathing dresses on it. The northern shoulder of Ben Tangaval was now the most astonishing colour—not orange nor peach nor purple but undeniably brown, yet a luminous brown raised to the power of *n*.

On Friday afternoon, which it now is, I am desolately waiting for my boat to Lochboisdale—due at 5.30 but will probably be late as it is the Glasgow Fair weekend. I have just been walking round the herring piers where nothing is doing. A few men were tarring the roofs of the sheds. One man was pouring brine into the barrels through a funnel, then replacing the bungs. Gulls were digging in some open barrels of guts. Hens scratched around a rusty gun, memorial of the Great War. I saw a trip to Barra Head advertised in the post-office. It costs 18*s.* 6*d.* return (Who anyway would take a single?), so I decided that it was not worth while waiting here the weekend for it. Castlebay seems as familiar to me as Marlborough or Merton College. I must get quickly to somewhere which is not familiar.

Writing this in my tin bungalow I overhear a drunken self-conversation in Gaelic from an old man lying on the hill at the back of the hotel. I look at my face in the glass and observe that it is tanned. I take a Capstan cigarette—the favourite cigarette here—and light it very deliberately. An unusual experience—I am reduced to killing time. Don't talk to me about the Isles of Youth. These are the Isles of Senescence, of Inactivity, Recovery from Nerves. For those who want a change from the hustle of the Office and the Underground nothing could be better. But I have not been hustled in the Office or the Underground. I do not want to sleep or dream of Tir n'an Og. I must certainly get on to an island where the roads are not merely circular. I want a day's walking without getting back where I started. They tell me that Lochboisdale is full of anglers. Well, I just don't care. I am ready to face any amount of fishing shop in order merely to get somewhere where I have not been before.

Vatersay yesterday was delightful but Castlebay, though not without its charm, is killing.

I am wondering what I shall have for tea, as I cut my dinner again. Am oscillating now between greed and sentimentality. Comparing Barra with the Island of Achill where I last was in 1929 while I was still an undergraduate (Not that I am in the least sentimental about my undergraduate days—a limbo period spent in slouching and fretting). Achill undoubtedly wins over Barra. But Achill is more mournful though not nearly so depressing. It was August. After walking the road through the bog which is full of stumps of bog-oak like bones, we heard a robin singing and someone said, 'That is its winter song. It is the first time I have heard it this year.' I left Achill and fled for the South of France. But there night came earlier and summer, in spite of the cicadas, was just as undeniably over. And every year since I have been terrified by the movement of the year. The buoyant months are May and June. Once they are over, I feel defeated.

When I was nineteen and twenty I was very excited if I walked up a road. Because, like a character in G. K. Chesterton, I expected some adventure round the corner. But now I realise that, contrary to adolescent expectations, adventures are not things which happen at random. The globe-trotter, the flaneur, the wandering dilettante of sensations, these are not the people who get adventures. An adventure must be important to the adventurer. You cannot collect them with scissors and a pot of paste. You must work for them. They must be related to your work and come to you in the course of it.

Farewell the castle in the air which never saw hod or trowel. I go round the Hebrides with scissors and a pot of paste. Quite amusing for me, and also, I hope, for others. But I need not expect adventures. Even if I fall down a cliff or am robbed by a Gaelic thug, that will not be an adventure. Merely an episode, not integral to life or work.

The *Lochearn* left about seven and the sun came out for it, flooding down Vatersay Sound. We passed the herring boats 'Energy' and 'Enterprise' and sailed east and north. I picked today's *Daily Record* out of a box for tobacco ash (the whole boat was in a litter having taken over a hundred Glasgow Fair weekenders to Tiree) and saw that Sheriff Inglis and Barra were again in the headlines. Two Barra men had been charged at Lochmaddy with maliciously damaging a melodeon after a dance at Northbay. The local witnesses in the case had been transparently unreliable, and the Sheriff uttered strong words on their lack of public spirit besides severely warning the culprits not to 'take it out of' any of the three witnesses who had deposed against them. One of the culprits belonged to Barra organisations called the Big and Little Stiffs which, it seems, encourage unruly behaviour.

I had a last drink with the piano-tuner, and sitting on a deck-chair in the stern wrote the following poem:

Leaving Barra

The dazzle on the sea, my darling,
Leads from the western channel
A carpet of brilliance taking
My leave for ever of the island.

I never shall visit that island
Again with its easy tempo—
The seal sunbathing, the circuit
Of gulls on the wing for garbage.

I go to a different garbage
And scuffle for scraps of notice,
Pretend to ignore the stigma
That stains my life and my leisure.

For fretful even in leisure
I fidget for different values,
Restless as a gull and haunted
By a hankering after Atlantis.

I do not know that Atlantis
Unseen and uncomprehended,
Dimly divined but keenly
Felt with a phantom hunger.

If only I could crush the hunger
If only I could lay the phantom
Then I should no doubt be happy
Like a fool or a dog or a buddha.

O the self-abnegation of Buddha
The belief that is disbelieving,
The denial of chiaroscuro
Not giving a damn for existence!

But I would cherish existence
Loving the beast and the bubble
Loving the rain and the rainbow
Considering philosophy alien.

For all the religions are alien
That allege that life is a fiction,
And when we agree in denial
The cock crows in the morning.

If only I could wake in the morning
And find I had learned the solution,
Wake with the knack of knowledge
Who as yet have only an inkling.

Though some facts foster the inkling——
The beauty of the moon and music,
The routine courage of the worker,
The gay endurance of women,

And you who to me among women
Stand for so much that I wish for,
I thank you, my dear, for the example
Of living like a fugue and moving.

For few are able to keep moving,
They drag and flag in the traffic;
While you are alive beyond question
Like the dazzle on the sea, my darling.

XI

BAGPIPE MUSIC

It's no go the merrygoround, it's no go the rickshaw,
All we want is a limousine and a ticket for the peepshow.
Their knickers are made of crepe-de-chine, their shoes
  are made of python,
Their halls are lined with tiger rugs and their walls with
  heads of bison.

John MacDonald found a corpse, put it under the sofa,
Waited till it came to life, and hit it with a poker,
Sold its eyes for souvenirs, sold its blood for whiskey,
Kept its bones for dumb-bells to use when he was fifty.

It's no go the Yogi-Man, it's no go Blavatsky,
All we want is a bank balance and a bit of skirt in a taxi.

Annie MacDougall went to milk, caught her foot in
  the heather,
Woke to hear a dance record playing of Old Vienna.
It's no go your maidenheads, it's no go your culture,
All we want is a Dunlop tyre and the devil mend the
  puncture.

The Laird o' Phelps spent Hogmanay declaring he was sober,
Counted his feet to prove the fact and found he had
  one foot over.

Mrs. Carmichael had her fifth, looked at the job with
repulsion,
Said to the midwife, 'Take it away; I'm through with
over-production.'

It's no go the gossip column, it's no go the Ceilidh,
All we want is a mother's help and a sugar-stick for the
baby.

Willie Murray cut his thumb, couldn't count the damage,
Took the hide of an Ayrshire cow and used it for a
bandage.
His brother caught three hundred cran when the seas
were lavish,
Threw the bleeders back in the sea and went upon the
parish.

It's no go the Herring Board, it's no go the Bible,
All we want is a packet of fags when our hands are idle.

It's no go the picture palace, it's no go the stadium,
It's no go the country cot with a pot of pink geraniums.
It's no go the Government grants, it's no go the elections,
Sit on your arse for fifty years and hang your hat on a
pension.

It's no go my honey love, it's no go my poppet;
Work your hands from day to day, the winds will blow
the profit.
The glass is falling hour by hour, the glass will fall for
ever,
But if you break the bloody glass you won't hold up
the weather.

XII

JOURNAL: HARRIS AND SCALPAY

I REACHED Lochboisdale in high spirits and got a room in the hotel which overlooks the pier. The sun shone over the island on to the loch and across the loch's mouth the Coolins were visible, a chain of misty peaks. In the eastern sky the moon balanced the sun—a mere white shaving of cloud-stuff. The hotel was full of anglers but I was pleased to get a room with h. and c. laid on, and an electric reading lamp beside the bed. In the hall was a row of deer-stalker hats hanging below antlers; the coat-hangers in my wardrobe advertised White Horse Whisky; in the smoke-room were green wicker-chairs and tables with round glass tops. I ate a large meal and strolled up the road that leads inland.

The moon was now turning from a pale husk to a luminary. Patches of bushy green oats grew beside the road. I smelled peat. The air was rich and warm, like cream. I decided that tomorrow I would walk from Lochboisdale to Clachan at the top of North Uist—twenty-one miles—sending my kit-bag on by bus.

Perceval and Crowder were delighted by this hotel. I found them on my return drinking whiskey in the smoke-room.

CROWDER: Well, I like Wills Crofts myself. He writes a good yarn.

PERCEVAL: Talking of trash I have done some more research on MacNeice. You often find that these literary gents were born and bred in Philistia. This was especially so with MacNeice. In the County Antrim, where he spent his youth, hardly any of the gentry read books, but there were one or two blue-stocking ladies who used to open bazaars. These ladies used to lend the poor boy the novels of W. J. Locke. 'Such beautiful style,' they said. There was also a folk poetess——

CROWDER: How do you mean a folk poetess?

PERCEVAL: You know—

'Down the shady mountain,
Up the garden path——'

that sort of thing. Oh, she sold quite well, I can assure you, and the schoolkids recited her songs at the local Feis.

CROWDER: Did MacNeice go to the local Feis?

PERCEVAL: Oh, MacNeice went to everything including the Bell Ringers' Practice. He had to do *something* with his time.

I did not like this conversation (it was so painfully true), so I turned out the light on them and went to bed.

In the morning I had my first bath—in water as soft as hypnosis—and learned at breakfast that I could not send my kit-bag on because the bus had already gone. And there would be no bus tomorrow, which was Sunday. I hung about for an hour, not knowing what to do; I could not walk to Clachan carrying a twenty-pound kit-bag. And there was no boat out of the island till Monday night. I began to hate South Uist—or rather the wicker-chairs and antlers which imprisoned me—when I heard that a 'plane was just about to fly north from Askernish. The proprietor, wearing a green kilt, drove me hurriedly over very bumpy roads, between yellow and purple fields and little lochs bristling with reeds and dotted with water-lilies, and past a life-size coloured Madonna standing on a pedestal in a garden. I paid £1 *7s. 6d* and climbed into the 'plane with five other passengers—a full load. We flew along the line of the west coast, long stretches of sand, passing on our right the chain of hills whose high points are Beinn Mhor and Hecla. Once more Benbecula appeared more water than land, but North Uist looked better than I remembered it, speckled with powdered yellow fields. We landed at Sollas where three of the passengers got out. The strait between North Uist and Harris was mainly green but amethyst where the bottom was rocky. We dipped for Northton sands, banking steeply. These sands are yellow and the edge of the sea was a crystalline peacock green. I thought how funny it would be to crash here—a good place if one had to choose one.

Two or three cars had come down to meet the 'plane and I got a lift in a saloon car driving the fifteen miles to Tarbert. It had come to meet one of the passengers, an elderly woman who looked like a farmer's wife but who came from Glasgow. She sat in the back with me and another elderly woman. Beside the driver sat two children—a girl and a little boy. Every so often the little boy felt sick and the car stopped to let him walk for a little and get the air. He suffered very stolidly. The two women talked about diseases all the way from Northton to Tarbert—'the doctor said nothing was any good for her but mass-adgin.' I arrived in Tarbert in time to have lunch at the hotel. The hotel was full and I could not get a room for the night, so I left my kit-bag there and walked along the road running east, on the north side of East Loch Tarbert.

Tarbert is unusual in that it has four rival Tea Rooms almost next door to each other, and several elder trees. The walk along the loch is attractive beneath knuckly hills. The day was grey and close in spite of a breeze. Vivid green oats grew all along the road in long plump patches like bolsters. Here and there was a red letterbox fastened to a telegraph pole—four collections a week. Having walked six miles to Kyles Scalpay, following the windings of the loch, I went into the hut which is the post-office and asked for a bar of chocolate. The postmaster had no chocolate but gave me some almost inedible chocolate-covered toffee. I asked if I could get over to the island Scalpay which lies opposite. He said certainly, but that I had better have some tea first; he thought I must be very tired after walking from Tarbert.

His house lay just above the loch, corrugated iron, which he was engaged in whitewashing. In the garden were two tiny rose-bushes, each with a large very elegant and perfect yellow rose, as surprising an apparition as a woman turned out by Schiaparelli. In the parlour also were two yellow roses on the mantelpiece but this time of paper. On the walls were two enlarged coloured photographs and the china cupboard contained Silver Jubilee and Coronation mugs. I was given scones, Kraft cheese and rhubarb jam for tea, for which the postmaster refused to be paid. As I was leaving I noticed wool drying on the grass. He explained that his wife, who was away today, worked at the tweeds and making stockings and socks. She spun, dyed and wove herself, using a wooden loom. But wool was terribly dear. He showed me some of the stockings and tweeds—one very fine, thick tweed (two blue, two white and the crotal) for which she was asking 4*s*. 6*d*. a yard.

I was sent on to the end of the village where an old man rowed me over to Scalpay in a very heavy boat,

Filling the bobbins

rowing with long oars. He asked four shillings for the crossing which was a distance of about a hundred yards. I clambered up from the rocks on which I landed, up a steep hill of grass bastioned with naked peat, and came in sight of the houses which are grouped round two long harbours. I passed the skeleton of a steamboat with its bows run up the shore and walked along diffidently, wondering where to ask for a night's lodging. This was easier to find than I had expected. The woman of the house was at first rather eager to send me back to the mainland but gave way after ten minutes' conversation. I sat down in the kitchen and talked to her husband.

The nations of the world, he said, were in for a bad time. Scalpay, too, was not what it was. There used to be four or five curing stations on Scalpay but the herring fishing was nothing here now. He remembered when the German Klondikers used to come into Loch Seaforth and buy from the natives on the spot. Now there was no work for the young men and they had to go away into the Merchant Service.

He was very interested in the Jews whom he greatly admired. In the old days there were several Jews came round the islands. By the end of six months the Jews could speak Gaelic marvellously. Einstein was a Great Jew. He had read his theory in Gaelic in the Church of Scotland Magazine but could not make head or tail of it.

Scalpay has a population of from six to seven hundred, no horse and practically no road. They were, I was told, given a grant for a road for a year or two, but the grant was discontinued. The road now ends in the air above a potato field. A very stony track leads eastward connecting the houses, a number of which are Black Houses. The lobsters which are caught on Scalpay are all kept alive in a concrete pool, and sold for fancy prices at Christmas. I missed seeing the lobster pool, but I saw the lighthouse at the easterly point of Scalpay, reached by walking across the moors. I looked into one of the modern flat-roofed dwellings attached to the lighthouse (which had assumed inside the atmosphere of a croft) and was greeted by a young man who took me up the tower. The tower has a hundred and twenty-one steps and the light is 350,000 candle-power. The former fact means more to me than the latter. It occurred to me, as I admired the glass lantern, cut in diagonals and bulls' eyes, that a lighthouse tower is the best modern approximation to the towers in fairy stories where princesses are imprisoned. For lighthouses are round and narrow and painted outside in stripes. A hundred and twenty-one steps and you come to a crystal chamber, which can even revolve. If I was filming one of those fairystories I should certainly use a lighthouse.

From the top of this lighthouse is an excellent view of the Highland mainland, and Skye with the Shiant Isles dominating the nearer sea. Looking to the left from Scalpay you can see Loch Seaforth which divides the hostile territories of Harris and Lewis, and the steep hump of a mountain called Toddun.

I stumbled back across the moor, leaping the wet patches of bog while admiring the pink lousewort which grows there. I met a man with a long bamboo rod going to fish for lithe. I also met an old man sitting on the ground with his cat. 'A Norwegian cat', he said proudly.

Its father had come off a Norwegian boat that ran aground and took to going with the island cats. When I reached my house it was ten o'clock and they made me some tea in the kitchen. There was an open fire burning in the built-in range—the range framed with green tiles, on the mantelpiece two large China spaniels and an old-fashioned clock whose pendulum could be seen swinging lazily. Also a large dresser and a framed text. For my tea I had two boiled eggs—boiled for three minutes—some very good scones, home-made oat-cakes, and a large hunk of 'crowdy' the size of an ostrich egg. 'Crowdy' is a kind of very crumbly cream cheese, pure white and with practically no taste; I had had it before in Shawbost.

I went to bed at half-past ten—a very unusual experience, and found that, though I am only five-foot eleven, the bed was much too short for me. I had a long night as breakfast was not till half-past ten next morning. Next morning was Sunday. Bacon and eggs; more scones. They told me that a motor-boat had come from Tarbert to take some of the islanders there to hear a sermon by the Moderator, and that I could get a lift on it when it was mended, for something had gone wrong with it. One or two of the people from Tarbert came in and were most warmly greeted by my hosts. The people of Harris seem demonstratively affectionate and tend to clasp hands and kiss. They all spoke Gaelic to each other with great rapidity and expression—in great contrast to their manner of speaking English. As my host said to me, 'We get a bit rusty in the English. We never speak it except to strangers.'

They only asked five shillings from me for my bed and board, but luckily I could make them take seven as they only had three shillings change for a ten shilling note. I then got on the motor-boat in company with about sixteen of the islanders. The six miles' run to Tarbert was most enjoyable, though the sky was intractably grey and the sea slate-coloured and crinkled. We passed through a school of many hundreds of puffins, bobbing inconsequently like infants' bath-toys. I am told that the presence of many puffins indicates the presence of herring.

Scalpay I remember affectionately. I was twice asked there if I bought tweed and that made me feel less of a parasite. Back in Tarbert I was only too clearly a tourist.

I went once more to the hotel and sat in the smoke-room—a quick switch over from the Gaidhealtachd to Princes Street. Ladies and gentlemen all had a Sunday morning air except one red-faced old man in a kilt who looked like Guy Kibbee (that sort of face is not adaptable to the calendar). They talked about the English service which they had attended and about the mint of money which is poured into these islands by the Government—a quarter of a million in grants from the Butt of Lewis to Barra Head. And one old lady said you should just have seen the Commercial Bank in Edinburgh for the Coronation. Beautiful it was—all blue hydrangeas and flood-lit.

During lunch in the hotel I talked to an English couple—very Upper Ten—who had also been on Scalpay, the home of both their maids. The wife had written home for a book on wild flowers in order to identify the many blooms of the Hebrides. They were here, of course, to fish, but so far had little luck.

In the afternoon I went a circular walk of at least fifteen miles, starting up Glen Laxadale along the side of the Laxadale Lochs. Sky and water were monotonously grey and mist hid the tops of the mountains, but I was in the mood for bleakness and quite happy.

Perceval and Crowder were not quite so happy. They stumped morosely up the glen, discussing the Scottish Sabbath.

CROWDER: You can feel it in the air!

PERCEVAL: Quite, my dear. Still it's an ill-wind, you know.

CROWDER: What do you mean?

PERCEVAL: I mean that we Britishers have every reason to be grateful for our puritan background. Otherwise how could we appreciate the naughty little figures in the foreground?

CROWDER: What naughty little figures?

PERCEVAL: Oh, you and me for instance.

Having passed through the glen I descended a track to Loch Maaruig which is an indentation of Loch Seaforth. Here is a small straggling village cut off from the high road and containing several Black Houses. I peered through the window of the corrugated iron school and read in large letters, 'Has Nat a nut? Nat has a nut but not a net.' There was also a railway poster of the beautiful Clyde coast.

At the end of the village of Maaruig is a burial-ground on an exposed knoll projecting into the loch and covered with long feathered grasses, now blown uphill by the wind. Near here I asked for a cup of tea and was hospitably received—a large plate of cold mutton with scones. On the mantelpiece were two China pekineses and again there were Coronation mugs. And again they refused payment.

I said I had been on Scalpay and they answered with pride that the country was much prettier round Maaruig. I said that I had not the Gaelic though I was Irish and they answered that I ought to have it because the Irish and the Scots were in many respects very similar. A woman brought in two baby starlings which had fallen down the chimney in the next room. These they placed tenderly out of doors to be collected by their parents.

From Maaruig I walked bang up a boggy hill to gain the main road which I then followed home, going to the west of the mountains which I had passed east of up the glen. There was now a keen wind which I found very exhilarating, having met little wind in the Hebrides. When I had topped the pass and was going downwards with the wind in my face, I began to sing various scurrilous songs, improvising words to 'Bonny Dundee':

'It's a blessed long time we've been out off the leash
With our je ne sais quoi and our je ne m'en fiche.'

Down before me appeared West Loch Tarbert. My spirits rose and rose and I decided that if there were always wind, the Hebrides would not be so bad.

Where the road reaches the loch it joins the road from Maaruig which I had walked in April after crossing from Lewis through the mountains. Here I met two men in blue suits, sitting on the rampart of Ardhasig Bridge.

They are coastguards whose work is to spot trawlers coming inside the three-mile limit on the east coast of the island. Nobody bothers about the west coast, they said, because there's no shouting there. It's when there are line fishermen on the coast that they set up a shouting.

These men worked in a disguised herring boat—'a kind of Q boat'. But any trawler could spot it miles off, they told me, because it was so clean and well-painted. They themselves had no wish to catch the trawlers; they were sorry for the poor devils, especially now that they were fined not less than a hundred pounds and lost their gear besides. And at this point they entered on the usual jeremiad about the fishing industry.

Scottish fisheries were just not paying. Unless something were done the fishermen would soon be all on the dole or the parish. And the Government was not behind them. It did not support them as foreign governments supported their fisheries. The newest herring boats dated from 1918. Most of the boats had been used as minesweepers in the War. The Government was going to solve the problem of over-production by condemning half of them. For even in these bad seasons the supply was greater than the demand. It was mathematically impossible for the herring boats to average a profit; only the minority of them could make profits.

I walked on towards Tarbert admiring the loch on my right. For the sun was now struggling to come out behind me and managed to throw slivers of radiance along the water. For ten seconds it came out full and the grey posts of a railing sprang into bone-white assertion. I reached Tarbert shortly before nine and slept the night in a house in the village. My bedroom had a small dormer window, neatly filled by a pink geranium flanked by yellow lace curtains. On the mantelpiece is a clock with a loud tick and a whirring and resonant strike; as I lay in bed I heard it strike Eleven, Twelve and One. My mattress was of straw and the bed too short. The seats of a sofa and chairs were lumpy with broken springs, like the joints of a pantomime horse. The sloping attic walls were covered with a flowered wallpaper. I liked this room very much. It is the right sort of room to work in and the only room I have yet met in the Hebrides which I should fancy staying in for long. I had my breakfast there also and felt very much the bachelor in possession.

Monday morning was solidly wet. My hostess stood in the doorway and watched a tinker's horse descend the hill opposite from South Harris. This was an event for no horses are used round here. Event Number Two: the Glasgow Comedian (whoever he may be) walked past—a short man in an oilskin who merely grunted when we said, 'good morning'. I imagine that all comedians are taciturn in private life. My hostess pointed to a little house across the head of the harbour. 'That's Compton Mackenzie's secretary's father's house,' she said.

I went up to the bar to look for colour. Tarbert Bar, already described, is usually occupied by half-a-dozen men, all standing about five foot eight, all wearing cloth caps, all talking Gaelic and all spitting. I talked to a little man who served on steamship lines and who told me—the great boast of Harris in distinction from Lewis—that the wooden loom turned out much better tweed than the steel loom.

The great event of Monday is the coming of MacBrayne's steamer. This time it was the 'Hebrides' which was going on to St. Kilda with the Earl of Dumfries. More important to me—it brought me three letters. It is vastly exciting to get letters in these islands. For a person like myself whose chief pleasures in life are liking and being liked, it is a dreary abstinence to travel alone in places where such pleasures are out of the question. Letters from my friends infuriate me because they are always either formal or stilted or brief or inexpressive or incoherent, or merely rude. All the same I look forward greatly to receiving them.

Today I went only a short walk on which I noticed three or four Black Houses with weeds growing on the roofs but looking very snug, set cleverly in hollows in the landscape. A Black House seems to me the most animal type of habitation which I have met, though no doubt kaffir huts and eskimo igloos appear even more to have grown out of the landscape and to be natural products of the hands rather than artificial products of the brain.

For the first time on this trip I had Scotch broth today, at lunch. As hot as Scotch broth invariably is but rather better than I remembered it. For supper, or tea, I had two exquisite poached eggs after which I went up again to the bar. Here once more it was nothing but cloth caps and Gaelic, and I soon came home again to find I had a partner for the night—a traveller in whiskey. I have hardly seen him as yet as he went out for a wee walk. He thinks Tarbert is the hell of a hole. I have now one cigarette left after smoking which I shall either read an anthology of modern verse or go to bed. But I find that if I go to bed early, I take two or three hours to go to sleep. It is only 10.15 and I long to be in London where I could be ringing up people on the telephone. At 2.00 a.m. the Earl of Dumfries leaves for St. Kilda to study the bird life. Forty-one passengers accompany him for the pleasure of putting foot on St. Kilda; they will return tomorrow evening.

There is a Gaelic poem called the St. Kilda Maid's Song which, like many Gaelic poems, has an eye to the main chance rather than to the Celtic Twilight—

Deftly my love can hook ling and conger,
The grey-fish and hake, with the net and the creel, O;
Far from our island be plague and be hunger;
And sweet our last sleep in the quiet of the Kiel, O.

They lit an oil lamp for me which, unlike most in the islands, burns by wicks and not by a mantel. I could not be bothered to read my anthology and instead finished a poem which I had begun at Lochboisdale among the ash-trays and comforts of the Sassenach:

The heated minutes climb
The anxious hill,
The tills fill up with cash,
The tiny hammers chime
The bells of good and ill,
And the world piles with ash
From fingers killing time.

If you were only here
Among these rocks,
I should not feel the dull
The taut and ticking fear

That hides in all the clocks
And creeps inside the skull——
If you were here, my dear.

After writing this I went to bed and listened for the whirring clock. Most good poems, I thought, are a collaboration between Jekyll and Hyde. With me it is mostly Hyde—self-pity, greed, nostalgia.

XIII

OR ONE MIGHT WRITE IT SO

WALTER PATER: As the traveller first approached that long line of the islands which taken collectively and by that easy synopsis of the popular imagination, an imagination which in its instinctive short cuts where science would take longer detours often attains a beauty of expression more proper to what philosophers call the coherence theory of truth than to that other, the correspondence theory, were called long since the Long Island and still are called so today, he felt come over his mind like a flush upon the skin the sudden excitement not untempered by sadness of the approaching *Terra Incognita*. There came before his eyes the marshalled army of the drifters, among which the steamers had all but superseded the sailing craft, but it was not in a manner of speaking his eyes which saw them; he felt them rather with that sixth mysterious sense which is lodged below the nape of the neck. It seemed to him then pondering as he did the all but imponderable quintessence of a special locality, so important to a man of his sensibility though drawn as fine and subtly as a spider's web draped on an Ionic capital, that this world which he had travelled so long and with a so often disappointed ardour, had now little more to offer. Leaning his hands on the rail of the incoming steamer, but withdrawn in his mind into that *adyton* which philology tells us is a place not to be entered of the spirit, he said to himself *Ave Ave—age jam meorum finis amorum*; he had not asked for this but he was glad that it had come to him.

D. H. LAWRENCE: She walked slowly along the road from Barvas to Ness. There were no trees, so she could not observe the sexual shapes of their vegetation, but the sun shining upon the moors assured her that all was not lost. The peewits kept crying, crying, as they chivvied each other with an interminable vivacity. The life of the peewits was a life which was not hers but it was a life akin to hers, a succession of white-hot pinpricks on the dark lining of her senses. Suddenly she saw two crofters engaged in peat-cutting. One of them stood in the ditch and cut the peats with deft strokes of an instrument, the other man received the peats and piled them up in a wall as if they were sandbags. The crofters did not look at her but she knew that they sensed her presence. Though their backs were towards her she knew that they knew she was there. They knew it not with their minds but deep down somewhere in the darkness below the diaphragm. A great joy filled her that the crofters should know she was there even though they turned their backs to her. The soft fresh cakes of the peat, fleshly as the thighs of a mulatto woman, called to her like notes of music. As the first crofter cut each peat from the earth it was like a note on the piano. And as the second crofter took the peat-cake from him, took it from its dark bed amid the tacit womb-wisdom of the earth, and placed it on the top of the pile in the hungry glare of the sun, it was like another note on the piano but a note higher up the scale and sustained with a fiercer intensity. Then as she looked at the crofters she felt afraid. She felt afraid that they might suddenly turn and look at her not with their diaphragms but with the intolerable male questioning of their eyes. The crofters were part of the landscape but she was something alien to the landscape. She knew that she was something alien, her flesh contained an alloy, she was something newer and inferior. If the crofters turned and looked at her, it would be as if the whole long sea of the peat moors were to turn round and challenge her presence and tell her she had no right to be there. Ah, but she had a right, she thought, reassured by the crying of the peewits. The shadows of the peewits chivvied each other on the road. They chivvied each other, the peewits, they turned in their tracks in the air, then they came down again low—low and low as if to whisper a message in her ear. She knew in her blood the burden of the message of the peewits and a new self sprang up in her. Not the self which she had brought with her from Glasgow but a new self and yet an older than any of the selves which she had known. A great joy ran through her blood like massed bands and she thought 'I am as old as the crofters. I am only twenty-two in years but I am old with the wisdom of the earth. I am old like the peat which has lain beneath the surface for centuries. I am only waiting like the peat for someone to bring me to the surface, with kind ferocious hands to cut me in blocks and lay me in a pile in the sun.' She began to feel a terrible assurance, an assurance that nothing would stop her, that she would always now get what she wanted, infused with the wisdom of the earth, with the quickness and fullness of the earth that cannot be exhausted. She took the little ordnance map from her pocket and smelled it gently. There was no need to open it or look at it. She knew where she was going. With proud female steps she walked towards Ness like a swallow flying north in the spring.

ERNEST HEMINGWAY: A man knocked at the door of the Black House. Nobody answered. The man opened the door and went into the byre. He went through the byre into the living-room. There were four men in the living-room and a woman. The room was full of smoke.

'May I sit down?' he asked them.

The men and the woman said nothing.

He took a box that was lying on its side. He turned the box up on end and sat on the end of the box.

'I would like a drink,' he said.

'Aye,' one of the men said.

'I would like a drink,' he said.

The woman looked at him and got up. She took a broken cup down from the dresser. She took a jug off the dresser and poured water from the jug into the cup. She gave him the cup and sat down again in her chair. The chair had a castor missing.

He tasted the water and put the cup down on the floor.

'I would like a drink,' he said.

The woman shrugged her shoulders.

'I would like a drink,' he said.

A cat came into the room from the bedroom at the

Peat-cutting

other side. It walked across the room on four legs.

'I would like a drink,' it said.

'Aye,' one of the men said.

The woman got up and took down a saucer from the dresser. She opened a drawer in the dresser and took out a bottle of milk. She poured the milk into the saucer. She put the saucer down on the floor.

The cat came and looked at the saucer. Then it dipped its head and began drinking. It drank as if it was thirsty.

The man who had come in got up.

'I must go now,' he said.

He put his hands in his pockets and opened the door with his knee. He went out into the rain. The rain was raining.

'What the hell,' he said. 'What the hell.'

W. B. YEATS: One day I came to the village of Sorisdale. I remember that I did not know where I was walking as my mind at that time was much occupied with religious and other problems. In Sorisdale I met an old man who looked like George Mair but without Mair's vulgar insouciance and he told me some old legends dating from before the Norse Invasion. He spoke in Gaelic with which I was not acquainted, and owing perhaps to this or to some other reason I only partly understood him. I have often wondered since whether he was not pulling my leg. He told me that the sea lay down beyond the village and when I raised my eyes I saw that this was so. Presently an old woman came out from a whitewashed house, and when she had looked at me for some time went back into the house and shut the door. I have no doubt that she thought I was one of the other-dwellers and that her shutting of the door was an instance of that atavism so common among Celtic peoples. It was not surprising that she was afraid of me, for at that time I had not been able to have my hair cut as there was no photographer on the island, and my eyes, as is common with persons on the verge of a trance, were enlarged like the eyes of a *revenant*. I felt, as I looked at the shut door, that if I had more courage or a greater conviction of my importance, I would knock at the door and ask the old woman some questions, but instead of doing this I turned round to walk back to my hotel, or rather, for all our actions are accomplished on two planes at once, to regain that equilibrium of spirit which human contacts disturb. I have often wondered since, when waking from sleep in the Reading Room of the British Museum, whether that old woman was really all that she seemed, or whether, when she shut the door, she did not retire into a more elemental chamber than the living room of her cottage. Such a question cannot be definitely answered though I have no doubt, since talking it over with an old man in Merrion Square who had once had tea with Parnell, that such a removal from the material plane to the psychic is as easily accomplished as the changing of gears on a car. The universe has seemed to me at moments like a series of Chinese boxes which we undo from the inside outwards. This was also the conception of the yogis and can be found in a modern guise in the poems of Lady Flora Barsac. When I stayed in her house in Hampshire, she showed me a poem which she had written with a wild goose quill and it seemed to me to be more profound, more exquisite, than the other poems of our century.

A. N. OTHER: All the time I sat in the *Loch Ness* I was thinking of the bridge below the scree. It was the first time I had come in direct contact with a murder. What alarmed me more was the thought of coming in contact with the murderer.

I took a stroll round the docks and carefully scrutinised the passengers. One of them was probably the murderer and that one knew my identity though I was unaware of his. There was an old man in a deer-stalker hat with a lump on the back of his neck. He was English and therefore suspect, for it was unlikely that any islander should have been concerned to kill that unknown little stranger, Dr. Fifield. The murder, it was admitted, could not have been from motives of robbery as a wallet containing £20 in notes had been found upon the corpse.

I looked round for other strangers but the only other passenger apparently who was not Scottish, was a Jewish-looking lady, rather flamboyantly handsome, with eyes like great black stones and fingers covered with rings. Having a good sense of smell I noticed that she was using the new scent, 'Ne Plus Ultra'.

I returned to my deck-chair and sat looking moodily at the Minch. I could not get out of my mind the dreary picture of the scree with the tiny bridge below it and that odd little figure standing on the parapet, taking photographs apparently of nothing. I had passed him at half-past three on that sodden and desolate afternoon (what an afternoon to take photographs!) and the murder apparently had taken place ten minutes later as the watch on the dead man's wrist had stopped at 3.41, owing no doubt to one of the blows from the sledgehammer.

It would have looked very suspicious for me but my action in at once calling the police as soon as I saw the news in the paper next morning over at Kyle must have completely proved to them my innocence. But they insisted that I should return at once to Stornoway as I was the only person who had seen the murdered man within three hours before the murder. They were especially interested in the fact that when I had approached Dr. Fifield he had jumped over the parapet of the bridge and skulked in the bed of the burn till I had gone by. One of the most curious points in the case was that they had been unable to find his camera, which must therefore presumably have been taken by the murderer. They asked me over the 'phone what sort of camera it was and I said that I could not see accurately at the distance but that it was a small pocket camera and being a V.P.K. owner myself I should guess it was a V.P.K.

A bell on the *Loch Ness* rang for the second supper. So harassed was I by my thoughts that I could not remember whether I had eaten the first supper but I went down nevertheless, thinking it was well to err on the safe side and that I should need to stoke up my system in preparation for the gruelling business of the morrow. It is an odd thing but even in ordinary life I often forget if I have had a meal or not. My family have always thought me terribly absent-minded and indeed there are whole half hours here and there in my life which I have been quite unable to account for.

I ate my supper with my eyes bowed on my plate; my thoughts were too unpleasant to make ordinary frivolous conversation. But raising my eyes to help myself to some salad I saw looking into mine those of the Jewish lady. Her black eyes were like holes into nothingness and from that moment I was sure of her identity.

Why the police should be so certain that the murderer (or murderess) should intend to trail me back to Stornoway and endanger herself by revisiting the scene of her crime I was in considerable doubt, but I supposed it was to sabotage my evidence which she might think sufficient to hang her. I could not see myself that it was sufficient to hang anybody but no doubt the mere facts of time and place would, when fitted together in their jig-saw, provide a clue which at the moment I at least could not see.

The Jewish lady having finished her supper lit a Russian cigarette. I could see that her hand was shaking. No wonder, I thought, but all the same a cold shudder ran down my back and I wondered if she had a revolver in that capacious though elegant handbag. Thinking of revolvers the thought struck me with astonishment that a woman should commit a murder with a sledgehammer, but looking at her again I saw that she had powerful shoulders, while at the same time I remembered the frail proportions of Dr. Fifield, and as I pondered the matter it all became clear to me as day. When I had approached Dr. Fifield he had jumped down over the bridge and disappeared from my sight in the bed of the burn. *But he had not been the only person in the bed of the burn.* There, crouching against the bridge where she could not be seen from the road, must have been this woman dressed from the Rue de la Paix and holding the sledge-hammer in her gloved but relentless hands.

At Stornoway I was met on the quay by the Police Commissioner, who asked me to have finished breakfast by half-past eight on the following morning and to be ready to go out to the scene of the crime. 'Did you see anyone suspicious on the boat?' he asked. 'Yes,' I said and I described the Jewish lady to him. 'There she goes now,' I said as she passed us wonderfully poised and leaving behind her a waft of 'Ne Plus Ultra'.

'As I expected,' said the Commissioner, and taking out his pocket-book handed me a small photograph. 'Found on the body,' he said. It was a photo of the Jewish lady—an extremely good likeness.

'Wife, or mistress?' I asked.

'Not wife,' said the Commissioner. 'Dr. Fifield, we find, was not married.'

'Well, was this woman staying with him on the island?'

'No, as far as we can ascertain. Dr. Fifield, you know, was camping, but we have made enquiries in the district and no one admits to having seen any woman about. We have also made enquiries from the purser and stewards on the *Loch Ness* but, as bad luck would have it, a whole party of German Jewesses visited the island last week and returned immediately. About a dozen of them, so it was no good asking if there was a Jewess on board.'

'Yes,' I said, 'I saw 'em on the boat to Kyle. I suppose she was there, too.'

'Luck for her!' he said. 'What about a drink?'

'Mine's a Haig,' I said.

I slept surprisingly well and met the Police Commissioner in the lobby of my hotel at half-past eight next morning. Hardly anyone in the hotel was up for the islanders are notoriously late risers.

'Had a good breakfast?' he said.

'Yes, thanks,' I said.

'Bacon and eggs, I suppose?' he said. 'They don't go in much for variety.'

I thought hard and couldn't remember if it was bacon and eggs or not. In fact I couldn't remember what I had eaten at all.

'Have you got a camera with you?' he asked. 'I should like you to take a snap or two of how Dr. Fifield was standing when you last saw him. I'll represent Dr. Fifield.'

'I'll get my camera,' I said. 'I nearly always carry it but I happen to have packed it in my suit-case.' I went upstairs, disinterred my V.P.K. from among my shirts and collars and rejoining the Commissioner we both climbed into his smart little Hillman Minx and rattled out by Stornoway Castle and into the moors.

After about twenty minutes I began to feel extraordinarily empty. Good gracious me, I thought, I don't believe I had my breakfast after all.

Coming round the corner of the hill from which the little bridge was visible, the Commissioner stopped the car and we proceeded to walk forward the remaining hundred yards from the corner of the hill to the bridge. About forty yards short of the bridge there was a heap of stones on the right side of the road. The islanders are always on the point of repairing their roads.

'Ah,' I said, 'that's where I noticed the sledge-hammer.'

'What? The sledge-hammer was there when you

passed?'

'Yes. It was lying on the top of the heap.'

'Then,' said the Commissioner, 'that will not fit in with your theory' (for we had discussed my theory in the car) 'that when Dr. Fifield jumped down over the bridge, the murderer or murderess was already waiting for him there with the sledge-hammer in her hand.

'No,'I said.

'That leaves', said the Commissioner, 'two alternatives—either that the murderer had a second hammer in his hand, which seems unlikely and further no such hammer has been found, or that after you had passed the bridge, he or she went back to this heap and fetched the hammer which you saw. I suppose you didn't turn round once you had passed the bridge?'

'Oh, yes,' I said, 'I turned round once or twice during the next ten minutes. I wanted to see if Fifield would come up again from under the bridge.'

'And you saw nobody, man or woman, on the road?'

'Not a soul.'

'You remember that the murder was committed ten minutes after you passed? And that Fifield's body was found in the bed of the burn?'

'Yes,' I said.

'Why, by the way,' said the Commissioner, 'if you were so interested in Fifield, didn't you look for him while you were passing over the bridge?'

'I suppose,' I said, 'I thought he was relieving himself.'

'How do you mean you suppose? Do you actually remember thinking that?'

'I can't remember, but that seems likely to have been

what I would think.'

'Pity you aren't more precise,' said the Commissioner who was getting steadily more morose. 'Now we will go on to the bridge.'

We examined the bridge thoroughly and the bed of the burn beneath it. The soft ground by the burn was covered with foot-prints. 'Most of these were left by my men yesterday,' said the Commissioner. 'Darn nuisance the way they blunder about. The foot-prints tell me one thing, however.'

'What?'

'There's been no woman down here lately. There's not a single woman's foot-print in the lot.'

'That's odd,' I said.

'Hm,' said the Commissioner, 'now we'll take those photos. I shall be Dr. Fifield.'

I took my V.P.K. and saw that I had only two snaps left to take.

'Hell,' said the Commissioner. 'You might have brought an extra film.'

'Sorry', I said, 'that's my memory again.'

'Well, we'll do what we can,' he said. 'Place me as Fifield was standing when you first came round the hill.'

I made him get up on the parapet of the bridge and hold his notebook in his hands as if it was a camera. Then I withdrew a little distance and photographed him.

'And how was he standing when you reached the heap of stones?'

'He went on standing like that,' I said.

'Just like that?'

'Yes, just like that, I think.'

'All right. Then all you can do is to photograph me from the other side.'

I did so.

'Now', said the Commissioner, 'we'll develop these at once.'

'In Stornoway?' I said.

'No. We'll do it on the spot. I have my reasons for this. Here is everything you will want. Now you see that sheiling over there? You can use it for a dark room.'

Dictatorial these chaps are, I thought. I filled a can with water from the burn and carrying my materials stumped up a marshy knoll and crawled on hands and knees into the sheiling. The doorway of the sheiling was less than three foot high and, as the roof was in unusually good preservation, the interior was almost dark. The floor was covered with rabbit droppings. I hung my coat across the doorway to make the darkness complete and set to my work. I laid the pan of developing liquid on the small ridge of turfs which supports the bed when the sheiling is in use, and slipped in the film. The Commissioner had provided a red lantern. A thorough chap, I thought. I could hear him moving about outside.

After a minute or two I took up my light and glanced at the films to see how they were progressing. I had little interest in any of the eight pictures on the strip. Not counting the last two which I had just taken of the Commissioner, they consisted entirely of snaps of the herring fleet at Stornoway and of women gutting the herrings on the quays.

Or, at least, I thought they did but when I glanced at the film lying in the developing pan, I dimly saw that those pictures were a different lot. There was the Commissioner all right but who was that woman at the other end of the strip who had been taken three times over. She was dressed in white and taken with a racket on a tennis court. I never took *those* snaps in Stornoway, I thought.

The middle sections of the strip were so dark that I could see nothing. They looked as if they would not come out. I put down the red lamp and sat tailor-wise on the ground racking my brains to explain the mystery of the film. Suddenly I got up and looked again. Yes, that was the woman all right. It was the Jewish woman who had travelled with me on the *Loch Ness*.

I leaned against the wall with sudden dizziness as the whole thing dawned on me. This was not my film and the camera was not my camera. It was the dead man's camera and *he* had taken the photos of this woman who had subsequently murdered him. She must certainly, I thought, have been his mistress and the motive therefore must have been jealousy.

But how had the dead man's camera got into my suitcase so that I had mistaken it for mine?

I thought very hard of the events on the day of the murder and wondered if, when I passed the bridge, I could absent-mindedly have pocketed the dead man's camera, supposing it had been lying on the top of the parapet. I have always been very absent-minded.

I heard the Commissioner moving outside the sheiling and called out to him—'I say. Something very odd has happened.' But the Commissioner did not answer.

I got up to go out to him, then remembered my

business and took another look at the film. Ah, something was showing in the middle section after all. This will have been one of the snaps he took in the rain. Maybe the snap he was taking when I came round the corner of the hill.

It was. There was the ugly scree, the road coming round the corner, and there was myself on the road just having rounded the hill.

This was Snap Number Five. Numbers Seven and Eight were of the Commissioner. Number Six was very obscure. I did not remember having seen Fifield take a second photo, but evidently he had taken one more before he was murdered. It was very important that I should see the details of this photo.

I moved the pan a little and watched the film steadily, and steadily before my eyes the picture came into being. This was the snap of a man at three yards' range—a man with a sledge-hammer in his hand. I could not see his face but his whole bearing was demoniac. I looked from Number Six to Number Five and comparing the figures realised that the man was myself.

In a panic I dived for the doorway of the sheiling and, brushing aside my coat which hung over it, began scrambling out like an animal when I realised that against the sky a gun pointed downwards at my head. As the gun roared and I fell half out of the sheiling, I noticed that the smoking gun was held in the hand of a woman. I passed to unconsciousness in the odour of 'Ne Plus Ultra'.

The doctors say that I am very unlikely to recover. If I do recover, I shall certainly be put in an asylum. The world cannot tolerate people who are absent-minded and commit murders during their moments of absence.

As for the Jewish lady, far from having murdered Dr. Fifield, she had come back in order to avenge him.

XIV

JOURNAL: RAIN AND SPORTS

I CAUGHT a bus going north from Tarbert at about ten in the morning, a box-like bus built to hold twelve passengers.

These box-like buses are as buses ought to be. There is nothing I dislike so much in a vehicle as streamlining; that is why I am so fond of the London taxi.

We went up through the mountains by the road which I had taken home on Sunday. The morning was fresh and misty. One of the women passengers was alarmed by the downward gradients as we descended towards Loch Seaforth. The road winds northward with mountains on the left and Loch Seaforth on the right. We had to stop when meeting other cars as the road is narrow. On these occasions a fat man with a fleshy neck poured out a flood of humorous invective in Gaelic; at least I inferred that it was humorous invective.

When we had left Loch Seaforth about a mile behind us I got out, leaving my bag to travel on by itself to Stornoway. I wanted to walk through the district known as Lochs, which is the south-east portion of Lewis. A road breaks off from the Stornoway main road leading to all the villages of Lochs—Cabharstaigh, Marabhig,

Cromare, Gravir, Lemreway. But unintentionally I took another road, marked on my map as a bridle-path, which leads merely to Eishken. Eishken, spelled on my map as Isginn, is not a village but merely a lodge belonging, needless to say, to an English family who come there for about three weeks in the year. More land is attached to Eishken than to any other lodge in Lewis and includes all the mountainous and uninhabited portion of the district known as Park. Here to the south of Loch Shell there live only four gamekeepers. It is one of the best deer forests in Scotland.

I had a very pleasant walk of from six to eight miles to Eishken, not meeting a person on the way and with the wind blowing in my face. It was a peat landscape with a background of mountains. I stopped once on the way to smoke a cigarette, sitting in the shelter of a peat-cutting and looking towards an inland loch.

Perceval and Crowder sat down grumbling beside me.

CROWDER: Swine MacNeice is. He likes this sort of thing.

PERCEVAL: I thought you were open-air yourself. Usen't you to play for Harlequins 'A'?

CROWDER: Ah, but then we had a ball.

I went on again finding the wind a luxury as it blew my hair back and inflated my oilskin. I was delighted to be annoying Perceval and Crowder. Loch Shell appeared below me with a chain of mountains rising behind it. Eishken on the near side of Loch Shell looked snug among trees.

It was about two o'clock and I asked for some tea at the lodge, a large house of three storeys. They sat me in a servants' hall with a faded wallpaper, patterned with yellow chrysanthemums. On the walls were three stags' heads, staring like docile Medusas. I drank tea and ate bread and jam and admired the garden from the window. Eishken has a hawthorn hedge and sycamores, a glass-house, many vegetables and roses. I asked the cook how I got to the next place. 'There is no next place,' she said. When I explained that I wanted to get to Lemreway, a village about three miles further east on Loch Shell, she told me that there was no path to Lemreway, so that I should have to get there across the moors. I started walking again about three. It had now begun to rain.

The moors here were a series of little hills and lochs, the going was very rough, the landmarks changed shape or disappeared. I was reduced to trying to find my way by the wind which was blowing more or less from the south. I passed a little loch full of water-lilies and climbed in succession two or three steep little hills of heather. The rain was now very heavy, and every time I reached the top of a hill and the full force of it hit me, I would stand on a rock and enjoy it as if I were bathing. The desolate voices of sheep, scattered grey among grey stones, I found exhilarating also. At last from a hill I saw a Black House near the shore on an indentation of Loch Shell and took it that this was the little village of Orosay which lies this side of Lemreway.

But I was wrong. The Black House was alone. A handsome dark-haired girl came out and walked a little way with me to give me directions, not seeming to mind the rain though she wore no coat over her dress. The collies too do not mind the rain here. They sit out of doors in a downpour, not bothering to move. I said that I should find my way easily and promptly lost it. Feeling more and more cheerful I gave up picking my way and began to walk straight through the marshy places and straight up and down the steeps. Chains of mountains or hills blocked every horizon, the rain went on falling, there was nothing but rain and wind, heather not yet in bloom, rocks, stones and peat. I climbed another little hill, and standing on another rock nearly lost my balance with delight when I saw down below me a village at the head of a narrow loch and the foot of a green valley. This was Orosay. It was flanked by emerald strips of oats and looked to me one of the most attractive villages I had seen in the islands. I ran down the hill, climbed a barbed-wire fence into grassland and followed a little stream down the valley. A red letter-box perched on a stump in the landscape. The Black Houses looked as if they had drawn in their chimneys from the rain. I looked in at the door of a Black House—the passage inside was ragged with rough stones unmortared—and asked my way to Lemreway. They told me my way and remarked that I looked wet. I was indeed wet; my grey trousers had turned mauve with it and my hair was full of warm water.

The path to Lemreway became a road and here I met three women carrying peat in creels. A kettle was boiling on a small peat-fire in a hollow. They were very cheerful and said *ladh fliuch*, which means, 'A wet day'.

Lemreway, like Orosay, is perched on its own little bay off Loch Shell. About half the houses were Black Houses, many of the others were of corrugated iron. I asked a fair-haired young man in the post-office if I could get anything to eat. He looked at me with much surprise, and said, 'Where are you going?'

'I don't really know. Somewhere up North, I suppose.'

'You haven't lost your memory, have you?'

'No. Why? Has someone lost their memory?'

'Not that I heard.'

'Well, why do you think I've lost my memory?'

'By the way you spoke.'

'Oh!'

He said some tea would be prepared. We waited for a little and then were called next door by his sister into a room with a wide white fireplace and a peat-fire burning in the middle of it surmounted by a large kettle. The young man talked to me about London where he has been several times on business. Two small children came in and stood very shyly staring at me. The young man failed to encourage them by saying, 'This fellow's come to take you away with him'.

I looked at my map and decided that I would try to walk to Balallan about fifteen miles. It was now about twenty past six. Having advised me not to try to get to Balallan they said good-bye to me with great friendliness. I put on my oilskin once more and went out into the continuing heavy rain, feeling much better after three cups of tea and three cigarettes. Empty rowing boats bobbed on the bay. No one came out from their houses.

There are many patches of oats at Lemreway full of dog-daisies. The strips of oats round these villages make patterns on the undulating ground of a type that people love to use in wood-cuts, though God forbid that anyone should make wood-cuts of Lewis. The wood-cut is a suffocating genre, suburban, alien to wind and open spaces. I trudged up over the moors and followed the road north to Gravir.

The whole road here was flanked by peat-cuttings, blackening the countryside. Stacks of peat stood out in outline along the edge of a loch. The road wound between piles and ramparts of peat from three feet to eight feet high. Occasionally there was a larger pile, shaped like an Aztec pyramid. I met three more women coming back from working at the peat; a wet summer means much additional work for the peats have continually to be shifted about. Feeling vigorous and almost hilarious I pasted back the wet hair from my face and sang several rather sentimental jazz songs, putting in the tremolos. I felt that I should like to roll up my sleeves and plunge my arms up to the elbows into the black soaking countryside. That I should like to find myself a giant so that I could lie on my face on the moors, kicking over peat stacks with my feet, drinking up the lochs. That I should like to roll naked on this country like a dog or a colt. The rain was warm on my lips and hair. The country though desolate was immensely sympathetic, physically comforting like the smell of horses in a stable.

Coming over a hill I found myself facing Gravir. Across a valley was a road along the side of a hill at right angles to my road, and on this road was a line of little tin houses at regular intervals, all the same size, but all of different colours, blue, green, grey, yellow or khaki, and with the roofs a different colour from the walls. It was very pretty. I saw no Black Houses here, so presumably these were recent substitutes.

Though it had been raining for five hours Gravir made a brave show also with lines of many-coloured washing. I walked along the road with the houses and was very angry to find that it was a blind alley. My spirits flagged and I walked the next two or three miles without singing. The rain had got colder and the wind, now blowing from behind me, more powerful. The rain had gone down my neck and up my arms and legs and the map was sodden in my pocket. After some time, however, I began to feel a hero and that got me along very nicely. And I thought of other occasions when I had enjoyed being out in the rain.

In my early 'teens bicycling over the moors of County Antrim; the water spurted gaily off the top of the front wheel as I free-wheeled down to Ballycastle. And at school sometimes at Marlborough running on the Wiltshire downs in shorts and a jersey; I used to love to get my shoes full of water, and would step deliberately in the puddles. And even last year in Seville, watching the Easter Sunday bull-fight, when the bull-fighters owing to the rain would not come on, and the audience threw their cushions into the arena. And when at last they fought and a man got an ovation, the Plaza, which up till then had been a circle of black and grey—brellas, suddenly flowered in white, thousands of handkerchiefs moving up and down like the circulation of cells beneath a microscope.

No one was walking on these roads, but another two women were throwing up peats on to a heap. They asked me the time and I said I thought about nine. 'Ladh fliuch,' they said.

At last the road swung to the west and I saw Loch Erisort with houses in the mist on the other side of it. I passed Cabharstaigh, and near Kershader, where the rain stopped for ten minutes, had a cigarette. Two little boys came up and walked along with me. One of them, pointing with a broad grin, said, 'That's the school'. The schoolroom had been gutted by fire, was minus a roof and one of its four walls. The rain began again, blowing on me from the left, from the long low lines of hummocky moors. The road passed between broad patches of oats full of yellow daisies. I asked in a Black House near Habost how far it was to Balallan? The Black House was very warm and full of smoke and humanity; plates on the dresser shone like moons through mist. It was about a quarter to ten and five and a half miles to Balallan.

I took my map from the pocket of my oilskin and found it disintegrating with the wet. I crossed a bridge which according to my map I thought was the end of Loch Erisort. But it was not the end of it by any means. Three times I said good-bye to Loch Erisort and three times it reappeared. The misty and sodden landscape darkened with approaching night. For a fourth time I left Loch Erisort and this time left it for good. Shortly afterwards, for the first time today, a car came from behind me. It contained two ministers and a lady and gave me a lift to Balallan where I arrived about eleven. It seemed late to ask for a night's lodging, but having been living for the last eight hours as an amphibian, and feeling also very hungry, I jumped over a gate which I could not open, and knocked at the door of a house. In the house was a policeman who was going to bed. He put on his uniform again and walked out with me into the night. We stopped at a minute post-office where I bought and ate two coconut cakes while the policeman went off to ask for accommodation from the postmaster's own family in their house in the field above. I was lucky. With great hospitality the family took me in and sat me before a warm fire in the range while they made me tea and a boiled egg and made up a bed for me. I took off my shoes and poured the water out of them. While I rubbed my hair with a towel, the postmaster talked about the War. He had been all through the War without a wound—first in the Dardanelles and then for two and a half years in France. It used to take him most of his leave getting to and from the Hebrides. He told me that he paid two pounds ten shillings' rent for this croft which contained seven acres, three of them arable. The standard of living in Lewis was, he said, much higher than it used to be.

I threw my clothes in a heap outside the bedroom door where they fell with a corpse-like thud. Next morning I received them back dried, ate a large breakfast, paid five shillings for my bed and board (they asked three) and ran down through the field in time to catch the Stornoway bus, for there would be no more buses today. In the bus I talked with a very genial Lewisman, who told me that ten shillings an acre was the usual rent here for arable land. At one village a lady in breeches and a beret, English, came up and spoke to the driver. My friend grinned a little sourly. 'That's the lady of the land,' he said, 'she owns the fishing in the loch.'

At Stornoway I claimed my kit-bag in the hotel and strolled along the quay. The narrow tongue of harbour between Cromwell Street and Stornoway Castle was a thicket of masts and funnels, gay with colour and gulls. As in Castlebay, women were gutting herring with speed and a beautiful dexterity. I was told that this afternoon there were to be the annual sports in Barvas and that buses would leave for Barvas once an hour. Though it was now raining heavily I decided to visit the sports.

I took a bus for Barvas at 2.30 and the rain lifted as we drove through the low undulating moors, diversified only by an occasional turf built shieling or a conclave of bags of peat, nodding against each other like drunk old men. The sports were held on the left-hand side of the road a little before the village and the cross-roads. A score of cars had settled on the side of the road. Several hundred people were talking to their friends. Three temporary booths were serving refreshments. A kettle was boiling in the open on a fire of peat. I paid a shilling for passing through a wire fence and looked round to see what was happening. Children sat on the crisp turf sucking ice cornets. The crowd circulated idly, happy in the newly-appeared sun. The air was very mild.

Beyond the River Barvas, to the south, the moors rose just a little and their long line blocked the horizon. By a mere accident I noticed between the crowd and the river a number of young men playing football. No one cheered them, and after a little they stopped. The ground was dotted with tiny triangular yellow flags. A man walked about with a megaphone which he did not use. All the young men in cloth caps offered each other

Capstan cigarettes. A Celtic timelessness suffused the scene like sunshine.

I smoked several cigarettes and bought some liquorice sweets. The people all around me were happy and voluble in Gaelic. After an hour or two a car arrived with some pipers. The pipers mixed with the crowd and talked to their friends, but revealed no intention of piping. Young men in striped football jerseys loitered round looking for an event. No events took place. The sun went on shining on the moors and the brown River Barvas.

I looked up and saw Hector MacIver in a mackintosh and a black hat. 'Where in God's name have you come from?' we said to each other. Hector was on holiday at his home in Shawbost. I was on holiday also. All the world was on holiday at Barvas. But they would not be able to have their usual dance after the sports in Bragair for there had been a death in Bragair.

Two little girls in Highland dress got up on a table and danced the Highland Fling to the music of the bagpipes. At the same time, after a long period when nothing had taken place at all, a long jump competition was held and several races run round and about unobserved. They told me that these sports had only been going two or three years, but that the organisation was improving each year. The two little girls got down from the platform and another two succeeded them. Hector said, 'Let's walk down the road'. We walked down to the cross-roads past the empty buses and sat on the grass at the back of the Barvas Inn, surveying a lively stream which runs down into the Barvas. Hector took out a quarter-bottle of whiskey. We drank it alternately and threw the bottle into the bubbling stream. Hector said, 'I hope the landlord catches that in his net'.

We went back to the sports and the hours free-wheeled in the sun. While the Highland Flings went on to the monotonous music of the pipes—two very gay little figures in tartan dancing in the air against the moors—the announcer announced through his megaphone that various people had won the hundred yards and the two-twenty. Throwing the hammer was begun. Young men in trousers and waistcoats leaned backwards upon the air and swung the long hammer round their heads. Half a dozen of Hector's friends collected and said, 'We will go down by the river'.

We sat where the river falls three or four feet in yellow foam. Each man took out from his coat a bottle of beer. The bottles circulated and, one after the other, were thrown empty into the rapids. A young man sitting on the turf, looking straight in front of him over the river, sang very naturally and beautifully a melancholy song in Gaelic. A man with his back to us made water into the river. Hector and I agreed that modern English poetry was vitiated by cleverness. The air was rich with the smell of the moors and sun and a feeling of a *bel viver* not dependent on wealth or cities.

We went back to the sports and waited for a car. We did not know if we were going to Shawbost or Stornoway. But there were no cars likely to go anywhere for an hour or two, so we went up to the post-office and had tea. After tea we found a bus for Shawbost and sat in it. It filled up but did not move. A fight began on the road and all the people skeltered to watch it from the sports. A lorry drew up—a travelling shebeen—and sold beer to the crowd at a profit of threepence a bottle while the police were arresting the fighters. The smoke still curled from the kettle boiling on the peat.

We reached Hector's house at Shawbost at about nine, drank some whiskey and had a meal. Someone asked me if I knew the history of Lewis and I said no. They said, 'But how can you expect to write this book if you are not steeped in the history of the place?'

I said, 'I have a slight conscience about that myself, but my public, such as it is, won't care if I know the history or not.'

Hector and I went into the field behind the house and looked at the little bay, Loch Sheaboist. The outer sea beyond the bay seemed to stand up vertical, a band of evanescent blue which shaded into the sky. The evening was very quiet except for a corn-crake. It was in this bay that Hector's grandfather landed when evicted from Uig, with all his chattels on the boat and not knowing where he was to sleep. All the houses on the left-hand side of this road were put up by evicted crofters.

Last night a number of casks of beer converged on Shawbost and many of the villagers were up till eight in the morning. Tonight there was a dance in the schoolhouse. We went to the dance at about eleven. But first Hector and I sat behind a wall and drank another quarter-bottle of whiskey. The schoolhouse was full, three rooms being in use for dancing; a couple of pipers played in one and a man with an accordion in each of the others. They danced only Highland dances, the single lamp in the room throwing wild shadows on the wall, upflung hands as exclamatory as the whooping of the dancers. The youths and girls were dressed as in any English dance-hall—blue suits neatly creased or grey flannel trousers; only a few wore their caps or had no ties. Some of the girls had dresses reaching to their ankles. There was nothing very *folk* or peasant in their personal appearance, none of Synge's hobnailed boots chasing girls' naked feet.

An old schoolmaster said to me, 'I could tell you things about Lewis in the old days that would raise the hair on your head.' Example: 'I've seen a man come in off the moors and take a plate of fish and potatoes, eat it with his hands and throw the peelings on the floor.' This failed to raise my hair. The schoolmaster talked to Hector about the decline of the islands while I, in a haze, watched the moving maze of the dancers. When a young man wants to walk out with a girl in the open air he has to invite her by a deputy. Many had evidently done this.

Some of the tinkers who travel round Lewis, are very good at the bagpipes. Hector says he remembers a dance when he was a little boy, where two tinkers sat on the window-ledge looking in, winking at each other and putting out their tongues at the piper. This dance tonight was the first dance in the village where he had seen pipers present dressed in Highland costume.

Hector took part in a reel and we went home, raked up the peats in the fireplace and boiled a kettle for some tea. We talked about the complexities of civilisation till about four in the morning, then went to bed.

XV

JOURNAL: DRIFTERS AND HERMITS

NEXT MORNING Hector and I both had to catch the bus to Stornoway. He wanted to get a permit to visit the Flannan Island Lighthouse, and I wanted to go out in a drifter. As we waited for the bus a man came over the brae with a large poached salmon under his arm. My heart rejoiced as it would rejoice when anyone in these islands poached a salmon from the absentee and alien landlords.

The bus drove casually off its course to make a few calls and arrived at Stornoway about eleven. Hector asked me if I had noticed the corrupt Gaelic spoken by the driver. I said that I had, for his speech was full of obvious English hybrids. The fault of Stornoway, said Hector, with its ideas of progress; they mix English and Gaelic and lose all definite personality. He would like to see Stornoway destroyed.

We sat in a hotel and drank double whiskies from eleven till three. I observed a small boy being ordered a glass of port by his parents.

Hector said that he foresaw within ten years the total collapse of our civilisation. I accepted this with the cheerfulness bred of whiskey. Not so Perceval, who had in a moment of forgetfulness ordered himself a cup of coffee.

PERCEVAL: To judge by this coffee our civilization has collapsed already.

CROWDER: I expect they make it in a metal percolator.

PERCEVAL: I hope you aren't one of those affected people who despise percolators. In no essential function of daily life is snobbery so painfully evident as in the making of coffee. All these Wordsworthian æsthetes who make it in an open jug with a wooden spoon!

CROWDER: Well, how do you make it?

PERCEVAL: I never make it. My manservant does that for me.

CROWDER: But what do you do when he's out?

PERCEVAL: When he's out, my dear, I'm out also. As a matter-of-fact on his days out I take him to the Art Galleries.

CROWDER: That must be nice for all.

PERCEVAL: Furthermore one should never make what one can buy from others ready-made.

CROWDER: Good Lord! and I thought you were a Marxian.

PERCEVAL: So I am. Marx and not William Morris. I can't bear the affectation of simplicity. It is wholly illogical to fight for the right unless one is financially incapable of basking in the wrong.

CROWDER: Good Lord!

PERCEVAL: You wait till I've spent all my capital. Then I'll have a conversion. Comme tous les autres—

If I could sit in a garden shady
With a Horse's Neck or a White Lady
And snap my fingures like a Turk
To make the other bastards work,
Then I should feel extremely hearty;
But, as it is, I'll join the Party.

At three the bars close, so we had lunch. At about six I heard of a drifter just going out which would take me on board. I hurriedly bought a half-bottle of John Haig to please the skipper, fetched a cap and scarf and went on board this boat which was called the *Fisher King* and was manned by an English crew from Lowestoft. Most of the boats in Stornoway are Scottish boats, but these had already gone out. The *Fisher King* was late because she had purposely run herself aground to get the grass cleaned from her bottom at low tide. She had a crew of ten, mostly country lads, unmarried. To come again in such sudden contact with Saxons was a violent experience. Their hand-to-mouth optimism, the attitude of ' 'oo chum, come and 'ave a look at this 'ere,' the jokes, the snatches of jazz, the entire absence of Western Island melancholy, the mutilation of Lewis place-names (e.g., Tiumpan Head turned to Jumpin' 'Ead), the hefty badinage, the friendly curiosity, the faces and voices—all this I found exhilarating, if vulgar when compared with the Gaelic speaking islanders. But not vulgar when compared with the commercials who fill the hotels of Stornoway. Some of the Lowestoft men had beautiful faces and all of them seemed to possess both humanity and humour. None of these three things can, except in very rare cases, be found among the richer commercials.

They ran up the mizzen and we went easily forth into the Minch. I was shown the place, not far from Stornoway harbour, where the *Iolaire* ran aground on New Year's Eve 1918–19. On board were three hundred Lewismen coming home from the War. Nearly all of them knew the coast and saw that the captain was off his course. Only thirty odd of the three hundred survived. Hector had been speaking of this disaster this morning. There were five men drowned from his village of Shawbost and the corpses were brought home by two beautiful Clydesdale horses. No Clydesdales had been seen in Shawbost before, and in the middle of the night Hector's mother woke him and said, 'Come and see the beautiful horses which are quartered in our stable.' He asked what they were doing there and on hearing that they had brought the corpses, was so terrified that he refused to see them and buried his face in the pillow.

It was a fine, if grey, evening, but chilly, and I went down to the engine-room. The regular stoker had caught his fingers in the engine two days previously and his place was taken by a tiny unshaven man of the Comic Cockney type. The engineer, a pink callow youth, sang jazz songs indefatigably. The cranks plodded. There was a cheerful smell of train-oil.

I went up to see them shoot the nets—eighty-seven nets, fifty-five yards each in length, making a long trail behind us of corks interspersed with the floats, big white or blue bladders. When the nets were shot we went off a distance to drift and the cook prepared a meal. We all climbed down into a small cabin lit by a gas flare and lined with eight berths with mouths the size of the openings to dog-kennels, and sat round a small table covered with black and white check oilcloth. I took up a pack of bent and greasy cards and cut in three for my fortune. The crew were at once seduced and each man cut in three repeatedly while I made up significations for them. The Ace of Spades pointing downward fell to the wounded stoker and, this being a card whose meaning is generally known, I told him that it meant a death. This distressed him considerably but I made amends by telling him that I was Irish. He walked out with an Irish girl called Josephine Mary, employed as a herring girl in Lerwick. The herring girls have a very hard time, he told me—a shilling for each barrel they pack; all right when catches are good but no compensation otherwise.

The cook came down the ladder with kippers and tea. The tea was very hot and sweet. The kippers we ate with our hands. Afterwards a young man played the 'Londonderry Air' on an accordion. The men discussed the sort of yarns they liked reading. The skipper said, 'There is a good one too called "Sense and Sensibility". He told me I could lie down in his bunk if I liked; they would take the nets up about one. Several of the men climbed into their bunks and I did the same. It was very close and hot but I went to sleep. The cook cried out in his sleep to the stoker, 'Keep away from that grave or I'll set about you.'

About one the men got up, pulled on long sea-boots, black or white, and wound red bands round their wrists. With comic grumbling at the life they went up the ladder. I put on my shoes which I had taken off and went up the ladder after them, feeling sick from heat and lack of air. The cold breeze on deck was delicious but I still felt sick. The boat was stationary, rocking from side to side cradle-wise. The men were having cocoa before setting to their work. I was given a tin mug of cocoa—one of the most grateful drinks I have had for a long time. It was scaldingly hot but I tipped it down my throat and revelled in the contrast between cocoa within and the cold sea breeze without. I was delighted to notice Perceval being violently sick.

The taking up of the nets must be very exciting when there are many fish in them—each net, I have been told, like a solid sheet of white in the water. Tonight fish were very few. Two men stand by the side of the boat, their legs braced against the edge, and pull in the nets over a roller; the other men stand down in the hold behind, shake the fish out of the nets and stow the nets away in order. One of the men at the side also hauls in every so often a float and throws it bouncing into the hold.

The nets came over the side empty. Every so often there was a big splash and one of those ten-foot whales, which the men called 'blowers', churned above the surface and down again, its tail, unlike a porpoise's, going stiffly down behind it as if cut out of a log. I saw dozens of these beasts.

The stoker came up and enthused to me about the country round Lowestoft—the church towers and the beer. While for two hours or so they went on pulling up the nets. The sky became lighter (there had been no stars or moon). The last net was taken up and I went into the wheel-house to talk to the skipper. Someone brought us in mugs of tea and I brought out my whiskey. The skipper complained to me that when fishing from Stornoway one was not allowed to go out on Saturday or Sunday evenings. He thought Stornoway a dreary place.

The catch had now been sorted out into baskets—eleven of mackerel and one of herring. The mackerel are very fine quality, large and firm, but nobody wants them except the Norwegians and Swedes who buy them for pickling at two shillings the basket. The skipper of the *Fisher King* allows his crew to divide any money obtained from mackerel. He told me that the greatest plague they meet is dog-fish. The dogs come into the nets after the herring and bite through herring and net together.

We sailed back to Stornoway over a calm sea and reached the harbour about half-past five. Three or four row-boats accosted us from the Swedes and we followed one to its mother ship which came from Hunnebostrand. The morning sun was behind cloud but the light broke through in a wide horizontal rift of yellow. Three pink streaks stretched towards us along the water. The Swede skipper having bought our mackerel, asked us all on board for a drink of Schnapps—pink and warm though not very strong. As the *Fisher King* put into the quay one of the crew asked me if I had ever been to Lerwick (which now has a lurid reputation thanks to local prohibition). On my saying no, another man said, 'I'll bet I know where he has been. That's Douglas, Isle of Man.' Sad that I could not prove myself a gay dog I said that I had not been there either. The three pink streaks on the water coalesced into a barley-sugar stick of brass. The stoker gave me his address and I went ashore.

I had hoped to find a coffee-stall in Stornoway but of course there was no such thing. Stornoway was dead except for the quay where women, gay-headed in handkerchiefs, were already gutting the herring and putting them straight into barrels. I idly looked at the names on the drifters—*Emulate*, *Fortunatus*—and walked several times round the town, only now realising for the first time that Stornoway is a peninsula; it has quay on three sides of it. The shop-windows were depressing, Woolworth's being the best of them. A woman's shop displayed blue locknit underclothes (no woman should ever wear blue underclothes anyway). Above the door of a confectioner's, called Capaldi's, there was a repellent model of a cornet heaped with ice-cream. Another confectioner was called Gabrelli.

I managed to get into my hotel about half-past seven. I had herring for breakfast.

I found myself very tired and spent the morning in a coma, occasionally going next door into Capaldi's for a milk-shake. Afterwards I saw a placard, 'Buffet Bar', and went up some stairs into a pretentiously modern room, which failed to be slick or chic. Here I had a sandwich and a Guinness for my lunch, then went to the Reading Room in the Public Library. The Public Library, attached to the Town Hall, was erected by a benefactor who returning to his native Lewis, thought he could forward the march of progress by wholesale dissemination of cheap fiction and weeklies. In the Reading Room, as already mentioned, I found the *Tatler*, the *Sketch*, and the *Cornhill Magazine*.

After a dreary hour looking at photos of the tweeded

titled with shooting-sticks and celebrities bleary by flash-light, I returned to the lounge in my hotel and read how an old man, whose nurse had stolen his money, described her as an Angel in Wolf's Clothing. The paper had repeated this caption in a headline, and I could not see any sign that they thought the expression an odd one.

In the evening Hector reappeared, tired after having worked his way to and from the Flannans. The most desolate place he had ever seen, he said. As he looked down through the crystal lantern the guillemots and puffins had appeared like peacocks; and very distorted in shape. We had tea and pickled herrings before going to the Gaelic Concert in the Town Hall.

The Town Hall was packed with about nine hundred people, half of them come in from the country. It was very hot where we sat in the gallery. First the Provost of Stornoway, Provost Smith, made an opening speech. The Lewis Pipe Band, seven pipes and five drums, obsessed the stage like gaudy grotesque vegetation and filled the hall to bursting with sound. Then the Stornoway Gaelic Choir, a mixed choir of about thirty members, sang a number of songs; many of them, Hector said, were imperfect in their Gaelic. Then came seven soloists, six women and a man. The man wore kilts; the women wore long evening dresses or afternoon-gowns, mostly of a flowered material and nearly all of them ugly in colour. The two best soloists were Miss Margrat Duncan and Miss Kitty MacLeod. Margrat Duncan who has had many years' experience of audiences all over Scotland and knows her Stornoway, was very hail-fellow with the audience and dragooned them into singing the choruses. Kitty MacLeod, whom I had met before at Skegersta, sang without accompaniment, very naturally and fetchingly. She once more gave an example of the traditional Mouth Music, to which the audience beat time with their feet. There was also a lady in an orange-yellow dress with a clarsach. Every singer in turn was encored. Then there was an interval after which a bearded, rather pompous, gentleman spoke first in Gaelic and then in English. Then there was more pipe band, more Gaelic choir, more soloists.

After the concert there was a Grand Dance in the Town Hall. Hector and I looked in at it while a Highland reel was in progress to the pipes. Then the pipes gave way to the saxophone and they danced fox-trots—rather jerkily as might be expected. The Stornoway girls dress up but do not make the most of themselves. Hector and I went back to the hotel where we talked till the proprietor and his wife got out of bed and told us that we would be keeping people awake.

The next morning I found and bought a copy of the *Listener* in a Stornoway stationer's. It contained an article by a friend of mine on economics and another article by a friend of mine on painting. I felt slightly re-established. One might deplore that one was not a native of Shawbost but one could thank God that one was not a citizen of Stornoway. There is a natural culture which can subsist without comfort. And there is a sophisticated culture which depends upon comforts. But when the deserters from the former 'gatecrash' the industrial world and try to live by its bread or its cake alone—its grand pianos, its club chairs, its blue underclothes—then one is presented with European man at his worst.

In the afternoon Hector came to tea in the hotel with a young man who was in Stornoway sanatorium with T.B. T.B. is very common in the Hebrides and the fifty beds in the Sanatorium are all occupied. We had a very merry conversation about religious conversions in Lewis. A conversion usually follows a hell-fire sermon in Gaelic. The young man converted hysterically confesses his sins, gives up drinking, dancing, music and even laughing. After a year if he has lapsed into none of these vices and attended all the prayer meetings and services, he is possibly allowed to communicate. The young men in the island are divided into sheep and goats with the flames of hell between them. In Shawbost there is a young man returned from America who goes round talking Communism and Atheism.

Crowder and Perceval listened to this conversation with interest.

CROWDER: Well, I think it's all a damn bore.

PERCEVAL: What is?

CROWDER: When people get extreme in their religion. Religion's all right in its place—

PERCEVAL: Nonsense, my dear. The whole point about religion is that it doesn't know its place. And one must have extremists, you know. One must have chaps sitting out at the end of the seesaw. It's no good thinking in terms in terms of the community. And a well-balanced community must contain extremist individuals.

About nine in the evening I shook off the dust of Stornoway and took the bus for the island of Bernera—

over an hour's run, on the west side. The bus drives down to a little jetty on the Sound dividing Bernera from the mainland south of it. You cross the hundred yards of water in a rowing-boat filled with people, boxes of food, bags, tin cans and collie dogs. I was met by my host who owns, I think, the only private car on the island (there are three or four vans to scour a dozen miles of road). He drove me to his house in the centre of the island, overlooking Loch Bhreacleit. Though it is in the centre of the island, the sea is only a few hundred yards away down one of the roads. For the coasts of Bernera are ribboned with lochs of the sea while fresh water lochs spatter the moors of the interior. I had tea and bacon and eggs and went to a comfortable bed after they had asked if ten would be too early for breakfast.

We had breakfast at a quarter to twelve. 'After all today is Sunday,' they said. Outside the window was Loch Bhreacleit with rocky moors behind it—a landscape like Donegal or Connemara. Two black kittens leaped up the window-pane after a blue-bottle. A small, ratty, short-haired, long-eared dog with Cairn in it (much nicer than a real Cairn) played with a large shaggy black dog who might have had collie plus Old English Sheepdog plus Newfoundland in him. My hosts called each other Mummy and Daddy. On the bookshelves were innumerable commentaries on the scriptures and a copy of *Her Privates We*.

While my host went to church (they go to church by the old time here) I walked to Tobson on the west coast of the island at the head of a long narrow loch. Here there were Black Houses with ferns growing on the walls, patches of oats full of big yellow daisies, a field of potatoes in flower, cornflowers, thistles, dog-daisies, meadowsweet, clover, and the district nurse on a motor-bicycle. Beyond the water were the blue and bevel hills of Uig. I returned home at three for lunch—an excellent soup made of potatoes and onions, followed by mutton and home-grown potatoes of which they were very proud, saying '*These* don't come from Canada'. My hostess also makes jam from her own blackcurrants and rhubarb. But the currants are late this year through lack of sun.

My host here was unusually genial and talkative. He told me that he owned the only pure Rhode Island Reds on the island, that he had a tremendous admiration for Hitler, that he was puzzled about the Great Northern Diver (the bird which has never been seen breeding), that with a rod a mackerel is as good sport as a salmon, and that hens in his belief have a language of their own like you or me.

In the evening I walked east over the moors. Bernera is an island of orchises and lobsters. They have several lobster pools but have not started filling them yet. I climbed up and down, up and down, over heathery and rocky heights, the skyline turreted with peat-stacks, watching the islands and capes shift their position, change partners and colour. I went into a sheiling with the roof fallen in and found fragments of a Gaelic bible. In a short time the herds will be brought over from the mainland and all the sheilings will be repaired. I arrived home hungry for a meal by the peat-fire. Then I watched the latest calf have his meal—a red bull-calf born on

Friday; he has to have fingers in the basin simulating teats and even so does a lot of kicking and backing, his short tail swinging continuously.

An Aladdin lamp was brought in, muttering sulkily, and my host asked where I had been. On hearing that I had been east over the moors he said that it was a pity he had not known or he would have told me to look out for the hermit. This is a Bernera man who was in the army, a champion boxer, then a quack dentist, then convicted in England, then convicted again and put in a lunatic asylum, now living permanently in a sheiling on the moors north-west of Kirkibost. Won't speak to any member of his family, lives by fishing and perhaps with some help from the parish. Reads and writes a great deal.

Next morning I again had breakfast nearer twelve than eleven, said I would be back for a meal at three, and set out to walk south-east to Kirkibost. It was a fresh morning and the wind from the north blew the south end of Loch Bhreacleit into white cuffs of foam. It is three miles from Bhreacleit to Kirkibost. I had been told to look up the Lobster Man there. The Lobster Man was already in a row-boat with his son, but they put back to the sea-weed-covered rocks so that I could go on board. 'Man, you have a weight on ye', he said. (I am only eleven stone but that may be heavy for the islands.) They had four lobster creels on board, baited with hunks of mackerel and weighted with stones. These were lowered to the bottom in the middle of the land-locked bay. We rowed ashore, took on five more creels, filled them with mackerel and stones and sunk them in the bay. The bay seemed now to be covered with bobbing corks.

It was half-past two and the Lobster Man made me have a meal in his house with the son and his wife and daughter. After Grace in Gaelic we had another very good soup, cold chicken and sago pudding with pine-apple, and another Grace in Gaelic. The daughter, a pretty girl in her 'teens, with a fresh and rosy complexion, is on holiday from school in Stornoway. I asked if the teaching was done in Gaelic (knowing that it was not, but one has to make conversation). She said, 'No, it's in English. I don't like English'; then added, 'I liked *Paradise Lost*. It was very good.' In the English course they read Addison and Steele, Charles Lamb, *David Copperfield*. Could anything be more un-Celtic?

The milk in this house was very rich and creamy and they pointed to a cow, supposed to be Highland but they admitted not pure, outside the window. The Highland cows do not give much milk but it is very strong. This milk certainly I could drink neat, and that is a thing which I rarely do.

It rained heavily on me as I walked home. I took off my shoes and sat by the peat-fire thinking how very sensible these people are to have fires though the weather is undeniably warm. At about six o'clock I walked out again to look for the hermit.

I walked for nearly two hours on the moor without finding anything. Whenever I reached the top of a height I put on my glasses to look for sheilings, for without glasses I tend to think a sheiling is just a formation of the rocks. There are many sheilings on these moors and I visited most of them but they were all roof-wracked and desolate. Towards eight o'clock I was walking down to a loch when I saw a man there fishing. I decided that he was the hermit. He did not look at all like either a hermit or an ex-lunatic, but I had already crushed any romantic expectations that my hermit would look like Robinson Crusoe. This man was elderly but agile, with a cloth cap, and healthy complexion, a moustache, breeches and gum-boots. He turned and faced me. 'What on earth brought *you* here?' he said. Certainly the hermit, I decided; he is suspicious and hostile. I said that I was a visitor. 'Fishing?' 'No, not fishing.' 'Not trying to get information, are you?' 'No,' I said quickly. 'Well, look at these fish,' he said, 'I have caught these seven today and I have caught eighty-five so far while I have been here. I got one the other day that weighed two pounds.' Seven into eighty-five: at the rate of seven a day he could hardly be the hermit because that would only mean he had been here about a fortnight and the hermit had been here for years. 'And a friend of mine caught one in that loch over there that weighed three pound nine ounces.' Pause. 'Have you no interest in fishing?' I had never done it, I explained, while he unconcernedly caught his eighth and threw it in the bag. I asked him about the hermit. 'A regular bad egg.' And he told me the tricks which the hermit played with the lochs and lobster pools. He advised me not to meet him—'You never know if he might maul you or what. His house (*sic*) is just over the hill there.'

He changed the subject and told me that he himself, a native of Bernera, lived in Stornoway, where he had a shop. He had bought himself a beautiful house for £2,000. But lately he had been losing. It was the fault of the multiple shops. These islands had always been run on the basis of the one-man shop. It wasn't right to send the money out of the country. I agreed and asked the way to the hermit's sheiling.

This sheiling, like the others, was set on a high and rocky knoll—just a few feet from the very top. From a little distance it looked just like a peat-stack except that it was buttressed on the side by stakes of wood. Coarse sods from the top of the peat-bog entirely covered the walls and roof so that the whole building was rounded like the home of an animal—no verticals, no horizontals, no angles. On the roof were some gum-boots, birds' feathers and a landing net. The doorway, about three foot high, was filled with a wooden door wrapped in sacking and sheltered from the wind by a barricade of peat-sods two or three feet in front of it. I made various noises to see if the man was at home. But he did not respond. I listened for him moving about or breathing but could hear nothing. There was no window to peep in at. He will be classed with the cliffs of Mingulay, I thought; I shall never see him. I hurried home, trampling on heather and orchises, in time for a meal at nine.

My host came in with four rock bass which he had caught from the rocks. The biggest was a very handsome fish, ruddy-brown, marbled with grey spots. I told him how I had failed to find the hermit. He said to me that the hermit was a very intelligent man and had discovered by examining the ashes of his fires in the sheiling, that when great heat is applied continuously to certain stones, gold dust is elicited from them. The hermit, he said, was short and always very smartly turned out with his hair brushed back.

Bernera was the last place which I visited and perhaps the most attractive. I said good-bye to Hector on the quay at Stornoway and boarded the *Loch Ness* with a certain sentimental regret. On the boat was Margrat Duncan, the Gaelic singer, commenting admiringly on the concertina reflections in the water. I tried to sleep in the Olde Pubbe smoke-room but found it much too hot. At three in the morning I stood on the deck and took my last look at the islands, quiet in mist and night. The moon had an aura like a peacock's eye, Venus lay on a low bank of cloud over Scotland, blue Vega was high over Skye.

When the train brought me down into the fat lands I noticed with surprise what an opulent thing was a hay-field. I read through a complete novel and four periodicals before arriving at St. Pancras.

Perceval and Crowder got out with yawns at St. Pancras. They were met by flashlight photographers, pressmen and stretcher-bearers. As I went by unobserved, carrying my kit-bag and even more shabby than when I left, I heard their last remarks before they passed on for ever—

CROWDER: Well, that's over and about time too.

PERCEVAL: Il tempo fa passare Luigi.

CROWDER: What's that mean?

PERCEVAL: Only that all bad things come to an end some day.

XVI

HETTY TO MAISIE

[NOTE.—I met my old friend Miss Hetty—on the *Loch Ness*. She has kindly allowed me to make use of the following letter which she wrote to Maisie Reynolds, the novelist. Hetty's impressions of the Hebrides are not always mine, but I feel that many readers may be interested in her point of view. Parts of the letter are rather personal, but I decided to leave them in rather than mutilate the whole.]

Aug 1/37.
W.C.I.

MY DEAR,

I hope you are having ever such a time in Kent. Give my love to Stephanie and tell her that Lady Garvin-Garvin wants her to give a talk on Spain to the Chipping Norton Lefters' Club. Lady G.G. says she once heard Stephanie on the wireless and thought she sounded so sincere. I said yes she was and also rather striking-looking. Lady G.G. seemed to think this irrelevant. I fancy that all the striking in Chipping Norton she likes to do on her own.

I have just been perusing a stack of reviews of our Memoirs from Greenland. They seem to think that poor Hetty is rather a passenger on it. Little do they know the time she had doing the proofs. And what cheek saying there is nothing in the book about Greenland. Let 'em go there, I say, and see what they can do with it. You might lend them your tent, my dear. If they come out of *that* without pneumonia, the higher English journalism has a great deal more stamina than I credit it with. *The New Parson and Parish*—bevy of second-rate sensitive minds!

You know, Maisie dear, the Hebrides are much too Gaelic. I couldn't understand a word of it while I was there, and yet when I got home I found I was losing my English. Well you know what George Moore said about Douglas Hyde speaking Irish being like a stream of frothing porter (which reminds me of Rona Dain—she was tiddly at the time poor dear—saying at that party that the drama was a stream of eggs through a basket) well Gaelic, you see, it bubbles around you everywhere just like a burn in the sun—some of them are the colour of port and do you know I saw a child of nine being given a port by his parents—and really it has its appeal of course like logarithms did at school, especially when it is sung, but the unknown was never my *forte*, and I must confess I am rejoiced to be back where they speak the King's English (and talking of the King's English did you hear that Nancy has been walking out with a don there—you wouldn't think any dons at King's had it in them, much less Nancy, but perhaps two blacks make a white) well really, my dear, it is a *pleasure* to be back among Saxons. The Celts (whom the Scots call Selts) are O.K. for Sound all right but Hetty likes her modicum of sense. Am dam doribhi Am dam dilliou Am dam doribhi Yng ang 'ille bhig—you don't know what that means neither do I. I thought of learning it from Flora but thought that would mean too much whisky. You don't know my friend Flora MacLeod—*she* found Gaelic very useful when she was in Paris, because whenever anyone accosted her (she looks awfully like a tart, it's only her Highland complexion plus usquebaugh but the foreigners think that it's rouge) she just replies to them in the fiercest lingo of the Gaidhealtachd which is just as mediaeval and even more effective than a chastity belt.

It was Flora really who saved my life but that's another story. What was the real tragedy, my dear, was my lovely Harris tweed coat and skirt specially bought to be in keeping—nine and six the yard mind you—and copied from a model in Vogue. I thought seeing that they made it, it would break the ice with the natives. But did it break any ice? Far from it. I would meet some venerable matriarch, fifteen stone if a day, and say with my most winning smile, 'What do you think of my tweed?' The V.M. would put on her glasses, and coming and standing on my feet would pinch my sleeve with her fingers and half my arm inside it. A long silence while she went on standing on my feet till at last I would think it was my turn, and pumping up my second-best smile would say, 'It's a nice tweed, isn't it?' to which the V.M. would reply, 'Aye but it's no Harris.' Shattering wasn't it but do you know what they did if I argued the point? They would tweeze out a tuft with their fingers and start unravelling it and they would unravel and unravel till they got right down to one little filament of wool. Then they would stretch out the said filament and say, 'Aye, that's it, it's *broken*!' Because do you know why Harris tweed is so rainproof? Because, my dear, the wool of which it consists has never been broken up, it's the very same length as when growing on the poor dear sheep. Well the natives didn't really take to me, perhaps because I argued so, so in the end I gave up conversation and took to writing in my notebook and that they liked still less, especially when I did it on Sunday. After all I must have looked awfully Sassenach—*fecemi* Girton, *disfecemi* Bloomsbury—and everyone in the islands knows that all the Sassenachs are crooks. And they think it just impertinent when one goes round asking for statistics. What I wanted wasn't statistics at all but I thought if I asked them nice and sympathetically about their rents they might open out and give me some folk lore. It turns out, however, that they keep all their folk stuff in Gaelic—I suppose it's being Presbyterians. An Irish R.C. peasant will tell you all his superstitions and not turn a hair in English, but the bonny MacLeods and MacKinnons are terrified of being caught out—it's all that old misnomer, the Free Church. The religion is just too terrible. Flora tells me that a congregation up near her saw their minister hurrying on the way to church and sent him a deputation to protest that the House of God must be approached in bottom gear. The Island of Lewis she said is very much divided into parties—the damned with a capital D and the saved with a capital S. The damned are all for double whiskies and the saved for double damnation. And apart from religion there's the food . . .

Gap of a few days here when I was going to talk about the food in the course of which I met Christine. Well

Christine, my dear, has been giving me the lowdown on you. She says that you're using astringents and taking foam baths but frankly, my dear, I don't believe it—not after all you've said. I never would believe Christine anyway—you can't believe girls who have that sort of robin-like vivacity—and when she went on to say that you, Maisie—you Maisie Reynolds the star among our lady novelists—were going to draw a line under your eyes to make them look larger, I said, 'My dear Christine, Maisie may have underlined a lot of things in her time but not her eyes, my dear. Definitely that would be too much.' You see how well I know you, dearie. Christine gave me a copy of that new paper, *Dawn and Twilight*, with a review of Greenland in it. By Evelyn Priest the man who used to write novels. It was not awfully funny I thought, but then I couldn't very well think it funny as Priest had no use for our book. I think he must be jealous of you for writing *Not Suède but Kid*. But to return to the Isles of Youth as Mr. MacBrayne calls them, or it sounds better in German—das Land des Ewig-Jungens (next stop Tirn'an Og) not but what they all live on old age pensions, I was going to talk about the food. The commonest foods in order of commonness are, my dear:

(1) Bacon and eggs—Bacon salt. Eggs leather.

(2) Scones—50 per cent of these badly cooked, 50 per cent rather nice for a change at tea but you get 'em at every meal and not for a change. (Not being a Scot or a Pixie I can do without so much carbohydrates.)

(3) Porridge—Porridge.

(4) Herring—Can be exquisite when fried in oatmeal but not so good with the innards left in.
(5) Mutton—We'd better pass on.
(6) Tinned fruits.
(7) Oatcakes—All right for ballast.
(8) Crowdy—Cream cheese, as white and crumbly as chalk. 100 per cent without taste.
(9) Carrageen—Blancmange flavoured with seaweed or more correctly sea-weed disguised as blancmange.
(10) I can't think of what (10) would be but see I have left out tea. But tea goes without saying.

Next point: Lodging—

Hotels of two kinds—angling and commercial (of course some commercials stay at the anglings but not vice versa because you can catch an order anywhere like a cold but fish are more particular). The two angling hotels I stayed at were really, my dear, quite sumptuous and full of deer-stalker hats. Some of the hats were on pegs and some were on heads and it would be difficult to say which were the balder—the heads or the pegs. But the heads sometimes belonged to brigadier-generals, whereas the pegs only belonged to the proprietor. The commercial hotels were nicer because commercials are only middle-aged whereas anglers are sexagenarian. When possible, however, I stayed in private lodgings. The great point about these is that they don't get up over-early. On Sundays not till about twelve, for they go to church strictly by the old time, daylight saving being against the Law and the Prophets. Beds are a trifle Spartan but mantel-pieces score heavily with ornaments all round the wicket. Ditto the walls with texts. Which reminds me I have just been reading an article in the *Listener*, by Fernand Léger, the easel and mural artist, all about training the public to like abstraction and how he brought joy to a wall. He does those stylised umbrellas on a single plane. If I were a wall, I would rather have a text any day. Well, bed and breakfasts, my dear, are from three-and-six. And they ask no embarrassing questions other than if you speak Gaelic. But I had one frightful experience—arrived in a house at midnight and taken in rather reluctantly by two women with faces that dropped like the weights of a grandfather clock—you know, when the clock's going to stop, I must say I wished their faces would—well these poor souls looked at me as if I were doom and said they would do what they could. There I was sitting tired out gingerly on the edge of a chair with bursting springs, a family Bible on the one side and a live stuffed spaniel on the other, well there I was listening to them walking overhead and moaning to each other in Gaelic. I was just wondering whether I should run for it when one of them came in with a face like the Book of Job, and said there was a meal next door if I did not mind it being simple. I did not mind it being simple but I should have liked it a little less dank—they must have kept their scones in a bog-hole. And you take my word for it, Maisie, and never have any truck with barley-bread. The walls were as dank as the scones and covered with life-size photos of Free Church ministers. There was a smell like the corner behind the potting shed where my aunt buries her cats. The second of the women came in with a face like the whole of the Apocalypse and said, 'I hope you won't mind: we're letting you have our bed but we've not been able to change the sheets.' 'Not in the least', I said, true to the traditions of Cheltenham Ladies' College. 'The lavatory', she added, 'is in there.' The lavatory was only there partially. The plug did not work and the hand basin had a large hole in it. I groped my way up to my bedroom. One of the women passed me on the stairs like a heavyweight spook—'This is a house that's fell on evil days', she said. 'Goodnight. I fear ye won't be comfortable.' Her fear was amply justified. The paper in my bedroom was peeling from the dripping walls, there were no curtains on the window, the bed was lumpy and damp. I turned out the lamp and lay listening to the noise of the elements, at least I thought they were the elements until they suddenly said Amen and lapsed to silence.

My other bad experience was when I was ill—that was a few days later when I had joined my party—Nicholas, Susan and Susan's girl friend, Fanny. It was bad enough being ill but I was all the crosser at the time because Fanny made a set at Nicholas. We were all, excepting Susan, staying at the time with a lady called Mrs. MacAfterwards—that wasn't really her name but it sounded like that. I came down to breakfast feeling that my head would split; my tummy had been on strike for days. 'I wonder if I could see a doctor', I asked. The doctor, said Mrs. Mac Afterwards, lived eight miles away, was not on the 'phone, and would almost certainly be out. But she was quite sure, she added, that all I needed was a good walk down to the coast. I looked out of the window at a landscape sizzling with rain. What a bore Susan was away for even a lady doctor is better than no doctor at all. I declined to walk to the coast, and Mrs. Mac Afterwards, though shocked by my lack of character, gave me a Beecham's Pill. It was all that I ate for breakfast, after which I retired to the parlour and lay on the sofa with a rug; a very eccentric clock spent its time striking the quarters. After a lapse of time Fanny if you please walked into the room in breeches all as if she was going for an early morning canter in the park. 'Fanny, my dear,' I said, 'have you got any aspirin?' 'No,' said Fanny, 'I don't approve of aspirin. I am going to go and look at the weavers.' 'Where's your horse?' I said clutching at my sense of humour like a drowning man clutching at a bottle. 'Horse?' said Fanny and went out banging the door. I fell back on Nicholas whom I prevented following her. 'Nicholas,' I said, 'you've got to get me that doctor.' 'What doctor?' said Nicholas who like all artists likes to pretend he is helpless. 'Any doctor you like,' I said, 'but if you don't get him I'll die.' Well, Nicholas said that he would and of course I didn't believe him, and as soon as he had gone I regretted having sent him at all as I should have preferred his company at my deathbed. All that I had as it was was Mrs. MacA. and the clock. Mrs. MacA. would come in, filling the door with her person, and ask if I was not feeling better. 'No,' I would say. 'That's very unfortunate,' Mrs. MacA. would say and the clock would go off like a clock that had been in a loony bin—'Fee fi fo fum fum fo fi fee.' Between them they had me almost loony myself when would you believe it, my dear, I heard the noise of a car and there was Nicholas with the ravishing vision of a doctor. And actually, my dear, he *was* a ravishing vision. His hair was a mass of delicate light brown curls and he wore striking check plus-fours with peacock green stockings. His dreamy blue eyes had a 'Come awa' to the hills' look in them and he minced across the carpet on well polished shoes like a racehorse. Delighted to be attended even for my sordid affliction by such an unlooked-for Adonis I opened my mouth and allowed him to prod my gums. 'Just getting a little soft,' he said, smiling seductively the while. 'Now tell me about your bowels.' Looking into his dreamy eyes with the mauve shadows beneath them I told him my story with pathos. 'It is the climate,' he said, looking up more alertly as Fanny came in in her breeches, 'most of the visitors here are taken that way.' I wish to Heaven Fanny was, I thought, wincing at the way she was laying on her charm with a fish-slice and fish, my dear, is the word for it. 'Well,' said Dr. Adonis, 'I will make you up some nice little pills—nothing at all violent—and you'll be fairly all right in a day or two. Only it'll be, I should say, a good week before you recover your appetite.' He said he would make up the pills in his own house eight miles away and he would drive us all there after our lunch. 'That will be a lift on your way,' he said. 'Way to where?' I said. 'That's all right,' said Nicholas who had listened with delight to the whole of my medical interview, 'I told him we were going to move on.' 'Nonsense,' I said, 'I can't move anywhere.' But the short of it was, my dear, that we all moved off, or on if you prefer it, after lunch, Mrs. MacAfterwards having told us in the meanwhile aside that the doctor was known in the district as Bonny Prince Charlie. The doctor drove us in his car, Fanny, of course, sitting beside him and me being next to Nicholas which normally, my dear, I should have liked, but he would keep smoking his shag. The doctor put us in his drawing-room while he went to make up some pills which he said wouldn't give me any pain but that of course was a lie. Meanwhile we looked at the drawing-room—double-endorsed comfort and a wealth of shot silk curtains. The walls were covered with photographs of wedding groups—I daresay he is a professional best man. When he came back we all had a cosy little chat. Fanny and I sat on a rather Dragey sofa, F. giving him the works and me feeling now so bad that I decided to scratch my entry. The doctor sat down opposite Fanny and told her of his tragic existence. Five evenings a week he said he spent at home in his house and no one darkened his doorstep. It was quite impossible in the district to make up a four for bridge. He had to drive twenty miles for a game of tennis or golf. 'That's terrible,' said Fanny who can no more play bridge than sing in tune. Nicholas was meanwhile walking round the room wincing at everything he saw. I saw that I must get him away before he said it out loud so I sacrificed Fanny's flirtation not altogether with regret, and said I was afraid we must get on. So ended our one romantic episode.

Dr. Prince Charlie was not, I suppose, very typical. Not if one goes by the schoolmasters. Talk of Patience sitting on a monument—if Patience ever met one of the island schoolmasters, she would take up her monument and walk. I met only two exceptions. One was a very nice man, highly respectable in his island, who goes to Edinburgh once in every five years and blows forty pounds in one. The other was a man with a red face who used to be I think a navigation expert. He was drunk when I met him and had a coarse moustache and a high level of incoherence. 'M'boy,' he kept saying to Nicholas, 'Funniest story y'ever heard. Wait till ye hear this, m'boy. Funniest story y'ever heard.' All about a skipper in the Malay Seas who was seasick. Last I saw of this worthy he was lying down in a field talking to the sheep in Gaelic.

I have met so many drunks in my time I would rather have met someone with second-sight. Flora MacLeod told me of a young man who had it in her village. This young man kept a shop and every so often when people used to come to buy groceries he would notice they had come in their shrouds and then he would fall in a faint. When he came to he used to say 'So-and-so is going to die', and die they did. After a bit Flora said he realised he was being rather tactless, so though he couldn't stop himself fainting he made it a rule not to say who he was fainting about. So after that whenever he fainted the village would be all abuzz with gossip as to who it was going to be this time. Then as soon as the next person died they would all run off to the young man and say, 'Did you know it was him?' and he would say he knew it all along. I told Flora that was a lovely story and she ought to put it in the Children's Hour from Edinburgh. She said there were many odder things than that in the village, so I asked her if she had any Firbolgs there, because there is something about a Firbolg that I have always found rather fetching. Flora thought I was pulling her leg and answered rather huffily that Firbolgs were prehistoric and anyway ought to be called Ciuthachs. Personally, Maisie, as you know, I can take the prehistoric only in very small doses. In Lewis they took me to see a thing like Stonehenge and, my dear, was it a bore! The avenue of stones is cruciform and is said to be aligned on Capella. They aligned 'em on Capella in order to know when to start the year. I am told that the Callernish stones are mentioned in Ossian. Personally I've never read Ossian, but I daresay I'll try him some day when I'm ill, along with *Das Kapital* and the *Bhagavadgita* and all those books by G. D. H. Cole and Professor Eddington. The first thing I did when I got back here to London was to go to the Galeries Lafayette to fit myself out with undies—that doesn't sound awfully relevant, but it just came into my head. In North Uist, you see, a place which was perfectly deadly, I went a ten miles' walk all alone with Nicholas. Nothing to see but lochs. There are said to be five varieties of wild goose, and Nicholas and I had a bet which of us should see the most, but of course neither of us saw any. So faute de mieux I hoped that Nicholas would propose to me, but Nicholas is terribly whimsy when he gets out under the sky—quite unlike what he is at a sherry party—and he took out his notebook and began making Scottish Proverbs. I should like to be engaged again since breaking it off with Robin, but Nicholas was so keen on his proverbs that I humoured him and laughed when I could. Well the only proverbs I can remember now are 'A Scottish face should be heard and not seen' and 'He laughs last who sees the joke last and ye can bet he's a Scot'. After that Nicholas talked about Nonconformity and how bad it was because it prevented people being physical, so I sat down on a dyke and said I felt tired. Nicholas sat down on the dyke and told me how repellent he found the Highland dances because they were so asexual. So when he had talked about sex in general for some time I hoped he would come down to particulars, but not a bit of it, my dear, all he did was to take out his cigarette lighter and ask me if I could mend it. So in despair I said that it was time to walk back, but Nicholas merely said all right and that the bet still held about the geese.

Nicholas really behaved very badly on this trip. Our last little treat in Stornoway was going to a Gaelic concert, and there was a woman there with a clarsach in a striking creation of deep orange-yellow satin. Clarsach = harp and Nicholas said she hadn't the figure for a harp and he would prefer it played by his saluki. Everyone turned round because Nicholas was speaking so loud, and he went on to say that Celtic culture was a contradiction in terms—if it was culture it wasn't Celtic and if it was Celtic it wasn't culture. So I had to take him out in the middle and give him a milk-shake in Capaldi's (fine old Highland name, what?) for Nicholas adores a milk-shake nearly as much as a gin. Susan and Fanny sat it through. Fanny said she thought it extremely interesting and when she got home she would buy herself some Gaelic records. Nicholas said she could buy hersel a couple of tom-cats and no one would ever know the difference. Fanny said there was no need to be vulgar just because one had been to the Slade. Nicholas said there was no need to be precious and go about buying Gaelic records just because one had been to the Royal Academy of Dramatic Art and had had to give it up for a teashop. Susan, who has a habit of never listening, said that she wondered the climate was not more conducive to goitre. This is just typical of all our conversations round the islands (the worst one was talking with some anglers who made jokes about corns when Susan who has no sense of humour, gave them a lecture on digital erotism). If ever you go to the Hebrides, Maisie, don't you go like I did with a female doctor, an artist or a girl like Fanny. Poor Fanny cut no ice with Nicholas. Nicholas said to me in private that she was quite all right below the neck but he didn't like the way she dilated her nostrils. I must say that I was a little pained myself to hear that the first thing Nicholas did on arriving in London was to look up that little bel pezzo of his in Hammersmith Broadway. As for Fanny she was livid, I believe the only reason she came was to get off with Nicholas, and all she got out of it was a septic heel and a box full of samples of tweed and a few dried flowers. She was always trying to get N. to compliment her on her figure, of which she is colossally proud, and her favourite gambit was to run down the Highland lassies by saying how extraordinary their figures were and didn't Nicholas think they were extraordinary, and Nicholas would say he didn't care a damn about their figures if only they'd learn how to cook, and Fanny would say, 'But seriously, Nicholas, I should be appalled if I looked like that', and Nicholas would say, 'Well, you would look like that if you didn't wear a Roussel belt', and then of course there would be a scene. It was terrible when she got her septic heel because it gave such a handle to Susan—Susan is the kind of girl who talks shop even in her sleep as having had to share several rooms, not to say beds with her, I can say from bitter experience. And talking of such things, Maisie dear, how are your feet these days? I told Susan that a friend of mine had feet which were convex where they ought to be concave and would she recommend operation, and she said no because feet like that were neurotic and the patient would only develop something else. And by the way about your astrology—we all know you were born under the Fish, but don't you think you ought to go careful? I mean from astrology you'll go on to palmistry and then you'll take to reading Jung. When I was in my second year at Girton a fortune telling woman told me that by the time I was thirty I should have three golden-haired children. Well, I'm going to be thirty in a month and I can't say I've ordered my tea-gown yet. Talking of triplets, Geraldine has mated her poodle; she had to set it up on books, one book under each paw. There was a terrible scene it seems because her aunt who was a missionary in India came in in the middle and one of the books was a prayer-book. Well, my dear, I must be off now to put egg on my face. Good luck to your foam baths—not that I believe in them anyway. I told Geraldine that rumour and she said she thought it was a bit much the goats stealing the thunder of the sheep—Geraldine is always so graphic. Well, good-bye, Maisie dear, take lots of love for your self and a portion for Christine and Stephanie. Let me know when you're in London.

A rivederla,

HETTY.

P.S.—Talking of *The New P. and P.*, Babette du Mortbois, the Fashion Editor, wanted you to write an article for her on Bavarian hats. So I said that you'd said that they were all so brilliant on the *Parson*, it would be throwing your pearls before oysters. So she made herself another cup of cocoa and gave the job to Sybil Donnelly.

XVII

ON THOSE ISLANDS

(A poem for Hector MacIver)

On those islands
The West-Wind drops its messages of indolence,
No one hurries, the Gulf Stream warms the gnarled
Rampart of gneiss, the feet of the peasant years
Pad up and down their sentry-beat not challenging
Any comer for the password—only Death
Comes through unchallenged in his general's cape.
The houses straggle on the umber moors,
The Aladdin lamp mutters in the boarded room
Where a woman smoors the fire of fragrant peat.
No one repeats the password for it is known,
All is known before it comes to the lips——
Instinctive wisdom. Over the fancy vases
The photos with the wrinkles taken out,
The enlarged portraits of the successful sons
Who married wealth in Toronto or New York,
Cajole the lonely evenings of the old
Who live embanked by memories of labour
And child-bearing and scriptural commentaries.
On those islands
The boys go poaching their ancestral rights——

The Ossianic salmon who take the yellow
Tilt of the river with a magnet's purpose——
And listen breathless to the tales at the ceilidh
Among the peat-smoke and the smells of dung
That fill the felted room from the cave of the byre.
No window opens of the windows sunk like eyes
In a four-foot wall of stones casually picked
From the knuckly hills on which these houses crawl
Like black and legless beasts who breathe in their sleep
Among the piles of peat and pooks of hay——
A brave oasis in the indifferent moors.
And while the stories circulate like smoke,
The sense of life spreads out from the one-eyed house
In wider circles through the lake of night
In which articulate man has dropped a stone——
In wider circles round the black-faced sheep,
Wider and fainter till they hardly crease
The ebony heritage of the herded dead.
On those islands
The tinkers whom no decent girl will go with,
Preserve the Gaelic tunes unspoilt by contact
With the folk-fancier or the friendly tourist,
And preserve the knowledge of horse-flesh and preserve
The uncompromising empire of the rogue.
On those islands
The tethered cow grazes among the orchises
And figures in blue calico turn by hand
The ground beyond the plough, and the bus, not
stopping,
Drops a parcel for the lonely household
Where men remembering stories of eviction

Are glad to have their land though mainly stones——
The honoured bones which still can hoist a body.
On those islands
There is echo of the leaping fish, the identical
Sound that cheered the chiefs at ease from slaughter;
There is echo of baying hounds of a lost breed
And echo of MacCrimmon's pipes lost in the cave;
And seals cry with the voices of the drowned.
When men go out to fish, no one must say, 'Good luck'
And the confidences told in a boat at sea
Must be as if printed on the white ribbon of a wave
Withdrawn as soon as printed—so never heard.
On those islands
The black minister paints the tour of hell
While the unregenerate drink from the bottle's neck
In gulps like gauntlets thrown at the devil's head
And spread their traditional songs across the hills
Like fraying tapestries of fights and loves,
The boar-hunt and the rope let down at night——
Lost causes and lingering home-sickness.
On those islands
The fish come singing from the drunken sea,
The herring rush the gunwales and sort themselves
To cram the expectant barrels of their own accord——
Or such is the dream of the fisherman whose wet
Leggings hang on the door as he sleeps returned
From a night when miles of net were drawn up empty.
On those islands
A girl with candid eyes goes out to marry
An independent tenant of seven acres
Who goes each year to the south to work on the roads

In order to raise a rent of forty shillings,
And all the neighbours celebrate their wedding
With drink and pipes and the walls of the barn reflect
The crazy shadows of the whooping dancers.
On those islands
Where many live on the dole or on old-age pensions
And many waste with consumption and some are
drowned
And some of the old stumble in the midst of sleep
Into the pot-hole hitherto shunned in dreams
Or falling from the cliff among the shrieks of gulls
Reach the bottom before they have time to wake——
Whoever dies on the islands and however,
The whole of his village goes into three day mourning,
The afflicted home is honoured and the shops are shut
For on those islands
Where a few surnames cover a host of people
And the art of being a stranger with your neighbour
Has still to be imported, death is still
No lottery ticket in a public lottery——
The result to be read on the front page of a journal——
But a family matter near to the whole family.
On those islands
Where no train runs on rails and the tyrant time
Has no clock-towers to signal people to doom
With semaphore ultimatums tick by tick,
There is still peace though not for me and not
Perhaps for long—still peace on the bevel hills
For those who can still live as their fathers lived
On those islands.

ACKNOWLEDGEMENTS

Many thanks to Bob Eaves, Head Librarian of Stornoway Community Library, Isle of Lewis; Bruce Hunter of David Higham Associates; Professor Jon Stallworthy of Wolfson College, Oxford; Professor James Knowles of the Department of English, Keele University; the staff of the National Library of Scotland, Edinburgh; Mike Sullivan and Jayne Miller of Barvas, Isle of Lewis; Juliet MacArthur; Hugh Andrew of Birlinn Ltd, Edinburgh; and Alison Rae of Polygon, with whom it has been a pleasure to work on this book.